# CARNEGIE HALL
# 1978

# KING OF SWING

**A pictorial biography based on Benny Goodman's personal archives**

with 212 illustrations

*Introduction by Stanley Baron*

WILLIAM MORROW AND COMPANY, INC.

NEW YORK · 1979

Designed by Lawrence Edwards

The publishers wish to express their gratitude to Mr. Russ
Connor for his indispensable help in preparing the captions
for this book and for allowing us to take advantage of his
encyclopedic knowledge of all things relating to Benny
Goodman. His own book, *BG, On The Record*, written in
collaboration with Warren W. Hicks and first published in
1969, is a mine of reliable material on the subject.

ISBN 0–688–03502–7

Library of Congress Catalog Card Number 79–84693

Text printed in Great Britain by Camelot Press Ltd.
Monochrome illustrations printed in The Netherlands by
Drukkerij de Lange/van Leer.
Bound in Great Britain by The Pitman Press.

# CONTENTS

# INTRODUCTION

Benny's father came from Warsaw in Czarist Russia, his mother from Kovno; unknown to each other, they made their separate ways to America in quest of freedom and opportunities – not only for themselves but for the generation to follow. It was in Baltimore that David and Dora Goodman were married, and over the next quarter of a century, they brought twelve children into the world. During that time the family drifted west to Chicago, where David found tailoring work in the sweatshops; but the family were poor, living in a succession of basement apartments, sometimes heated, sometimes not. Earning $20 a week at best, and occasionally out of work in bad seasons, David Goodman could provide only a precarious life for his wife and children.

Their world was more or less bound by the ghetto of Chicago, on the West Side not far from Garfield Park. As soon as each child was old enough, Dora Goodman encouraged him or her to look for work. The money brought in by the children began to ease the family's constricting poverty. The father was even able to entertain the hope that some of the Goodman children might rise in the world.

On Sundays, his only day of rest the whole year round, he would take the youngest ones to hear the free band concerts in Douglas Park. On one of those Sundays he discovered, in the Kehelah Jacob Synagogue, a rehearsing band of youngsters, and learned that any boys who joined would receive basic music lessons for a quarter. David Goodman insisted that his three youngest sons enroll as soon as possible. Performing in the open air, as bands did, would be good for their health; they might one day even find out that there was money to be made from music; best of all, perhaps, was the prospect of handsome uniforms, with metal buttons and feathered hats. The boys, of course, joined.

Harry, aged twelve, was given a tuba to play. Freddie, eleven, received a trumpet. Benny, only ten, required something a little lighter, and the bandmaster lent him a small clarinet. Years later, Benny's brothers said that he immediately embraced the instrument as if it were a precious treasure, with its shiny keys, its little green felt stoppers, and the parts that could be screwed together and unscrewed.

Although the Kehelah Jacob band soon suspended operations because of lack of funds, the three brothers managed to join the band at Hull House, the famous settlement house established by the admirable Jane Addams. In winter, their father would transport them through the icy darkness on the only vehicle he could afford: a sled from the junkyard. Trudging in front of the sled, pulling the rope, he hauled the boys along the streets to the door of Hull House. He seemed to believe, or at least to hope, that music might some day become the boys' escape route from the gritty world under the El.

But no musician could get very far without proper instruction. The person who, at that time, did most to put Benny on the right path technically was a white-thatched German of the old school whose name was Franz Schoepp. He would stare over his spectacles, wag a forefinger in time to each exercise, and generally make a boy feel small and serious. Although Germany had just lost a major war, Schoepp insisted that German culture would yet save Europe from self-destruction. Meanwhile, even through the terrible Chicago race riots of 1919, Schoepp gave music lessons to anyone – black or white – who was able to pay his very modest fee.

Among Schoepp's prize pupils were Jimmy Noone, Buster Bailey and Benny. Benny and Buster played duets under Schoepp's frosty eye, and neither of them thought about the fact that Benny was white and Buster black. Nor did it trouble them that the very music they played was split into hostile camps.

At Lutheran church picnics in summertime, the Hull House band were enlisted to perform the overture *Poet And Peasant, Under The Double Eagle,* and other European pop numbers of the same sort. After their musical contribution the boys gorged themselves with all the frankfurters, potato salad and cake they could hold, and trailed away to a rendezvous in the woods. There they would jam Dixieland style until the sun went down. *Wabash Blues* and *Darktown Strutters' Ball,* played in imitation of the New Orleans Rhythm Kings, were their favorite jazz tunes. Riding home on the El through the dusk after those long Sunday celebrations, Benny would often fall fast asleep. His brothers Harry and Freddie took turns carrying him home from the station to bed.

'Inspiration comes from within,' Schoepp used to say. He concentrated on technique, steering Benny through the standard lessons of Baerman, Klose and Cavallini. A group of Schoepp's pupils once gave a concert at a grammar school on the North Side; since Benny was among them, David Goodman and Benny's sister Ida went to the performance. Afterwards, old Mr. Schoepp embraced Benny, Ida and David Goodman, each in turn. Taking Benny's father aside, he confided that the boy showed promise of becoming a fine clarinetist. Schoepp even went so far as to add that he had great hopes for Benny's future. That compliment, Benny realized long afterwards, meant more than any other he received in his lifetime. It had signalled a small but none the less real triumph over crushing odds. Not Benny's triumph, but his father's — and that was the whole point.

When Benny reached the age of eleven or twelve, his father brought home a second-hand Victrola with a horn. This came with a number of records, and among them was one with a clarinet solo by Ted Lewis. Benny was fascinated by this; he listened to it by the hour and learned to imitate the whole performance, note by note. His father used to take him to meetings of a group called the Workmen's Circle, sometimes on Sunday evenings; and on one such occasion Benny performed his Ted Lewis imitation.

This led to his first professional stint, a similar performance on a Saturday afternoon vaudeville show at the Central Park Theater on Roosevelt Road. Benny went dressed in what were called short pants at that time, but were really knickers which buckled just below the knee. He also wore a Buster Brown collar and floppy bow tie. Inside that outfit, and holding what seemed an enormous clarinet, was a frightened but determined child who weighed no more than seventy-five pounds. He played *When My Baby Smiles At Me, I Never Knew I Could Love Anybody* and *St. Louis Blues* (if Benny's memory serves him), and was paid five dollars – more than his father earned in ten hours of button-sewing.

By the time he was thirteen, Benny began to get more lucrative dance band jobs. At first he played mainly in Murph Podolsky's band. They provided music at amusement parks, at house parties, at high-school proms, and even once or twice at Northwestern University and the University of Chicago. Band members had to produce musicians' union cards on demand, which might have posed a problem for Benny. Despite his youth, however, he succeeded in joining the union. He also bought an alto sax in order to double his usefulness and earning capacities.

The Podolsky band was high on enthusiasm, but limited in ability. This was brought home to them one night, in a rather startling way, at Colt's Electric Park. It was the Fourth of July, a special holiday night, and for the occasion a small pick-up black band had been brought in. The idea was that Murph's boys would alternate with the others to provide continuous music for dancing. But as soon as the audience heard the black group play, they wanted nothing more to do with Murph's outfit. Murph was naturally chagrined, and indeed furious. For Benny, however, that night proved to be a particularly joyous experience. He stood rapt, listening to the victorious rivals of Murph's band. Lil Hardin, later to be Mrs. Louis Armstrong, was on piano. The Dodds brothers – Baby on drums, and Johnny playing his sweet and individual clarinet – especially enchanted Benny.

**H**is sister Ethel was at that time employed as a bookkeeper in a men's clothing firm. Thus it was natural that Benny should confide to her his longing for a tuxedo. He was certain that a tux would greatly enhance his professional image. But Ethel protested that he was far too small: the shop couldn't possibly have a suit to fit him. Benny was nevertheless convinced he had to have one. Ethel finally took him down to the shop and induced one of the workers there to tailor a tuxedo especially for him. She paid for it out of her own salary.

Benny often had to work late at night. That was especially the case when Murph managed to book the band out of town at such places in the Chicago area as Evanston and Waukegan. Arriving home around dawn, Benny would stretch out on the living-room couch for an hour or so before getting up again to go to school.

He was a boy doing a man's work. The trouble, if it could be called trouble, was as simple as that. At home, even decked out in his tuxedo, he was still a child, and treated as one. It was no wonder that he felt lonely, not to say frustrated, at times. On the job, for example, between sets, when the other musicians strolled away to refresh themselves with alcoholic drinks and to talk about girls, Benny was at a loss. While actually playing music, however, he was the peer of anyone there. The result was that he concentrated more than the others. There was nothing he would rather do than play music – then, or indeed now.

An important date in Benny's early life was the 8th of August 1923. On that morning he had an emergency call from a bandleader named Bill Grimm, whose orchestra played on the day-excursion boat that plied between Chicago and Michigan City. Grimm's clarinetist had reported sick, and he wondered whether Benny could substitute. Benny was naturally delighted to oblige and went down early in the day to the dock where the boat was moored. The bandstand on the steamer deck was still deserted at that hour, although some of the instruments had already been set up. As Benny stepped on to the stand, he heard a shout: 'Get off there, kid! Stop that fooling around!' Turning slowly, Benny found himself eye to eye with a reckless-looking youth some four or five years older than himself. The newcomer carried a trumpet which flashed in the sunshine. He looked Benny up and down disdainfully. Benny, who was wearing knickers and was acutely aware of the other fellow's stare, tried to explain himself, but the trumpet man was in no mood to believe him. Fortunately, Grimm arrived before actual trouble could break out, and introduced them: 'Benny, shake hands with Bix!'

About half an hour later was the historic moment when Benny first actually heard the great Bix Beiderbecke blow his horn. Many good times and a barrelful of wonderful music stemmed from that first session on the lake together. One could never tell where music would take Bix, and so, while he lived, Benny listened with intent ears and all his heart to find out. Then later on, after Bix's early death, Benny listened every now and then to the few records which had featured Bix. They were still surprising, even after Benny believed he had familiarized himself with the dazzling butterfly lilt and dip of the notes which Bix seemed to blow in all directions at once.

But that started more than half a century ago, at the same time that Benny and his high school pals were collectively known as the 'Wild West Side Mob'. This title referred not to their behavior, but to their musical style. Unlike Benny himself, most of his friends played only by ear; at that stage they could not read music. Their jazz playing was burr-edged, free, ragged, but unflaggingly enthusiastic. This made them ideal companions in a jam session, but it also meant they had a hard time finding work. The commercial dance bands of the period used very little hot music, and then only as a frill for the sweeter stuff. Benny, thanks to study and practice, could play sweet, cool, smooth dance music on demand, and that meant that he could get plenty of work. But what he really enjoyed was to play hot, like his friends.

The list of young Chicagoans in Benny's generation who were to achieve lasting fame as jazz musicians is long. It included Frank Teschemacher, George Wettling, Pee Wee Russell, Joe Sullivan, Jim Lannigan, Eddie Condon, Bud Freeman, Gene Krupa, Muggsy Spanier, Davey Tough, Jimmy McPartland and many more. Benny did not know every one of them personally at that time, but sooner or later all their paths were bound to cross. They met to jam, and also to listen. Some evenings they would ramble around Chicago in groups to hear their favorite performers. On Benny's nights off from playing dance music, he and his brother Harry would join those excursions, which often lasted until dawn. There was so much to hear in Chicago in those days. For example, the miraculous trumpet of Louis Armstrong: Benny remembers only in a shadowy way the Vendome Theater and the Sunset Club where Louis used to play, but the great man's music of those distant times comes back to him even today as strong and clear as ever.

Together, Harry and Benny grew to know Chicago at night. It was a world of bathtub gin, redolent weed, Irish cops, Italian gang-sters, ice-cream pants, double-breasted blazers, raccoon coats, hot music pouring from golden doorways into the snowy streets, high black limousines, sudden brawls and shootings, and girls with spit curls who wore slinky dresses above the knee. In those speakeasy years, Chicago at night was a magical melting pot, and music supplied the fire under it. One night the boys could go to the Regal Theater to catch Fats Waller's act. The next it might be the Elite Club to hear Earl Hines on piano. At Thirty-Fifth Street and Indiana Avenue, in a tiny dive called the Entertainers' Cafe, they would call in to find Bessie Smith booming out her broad and boozy blues. And down at Thirty-First and Gordon Avenue, King Oliver, the Dodds brothers, with Bill Johnson on bass, would be rocking the vast Lincoln Gardens. At the Lorraine, it was Lil Hardin on piano, Buster Bailey on clarinet, and Freddie Keppard on trumpet. Keppard played with a handkerchief draped over his fingers; he meant to take the secrets of his music with him to the silence of the grave.

Eventually Benny found steady employment at Guyon's Paradise, in a dull dance band run by Jules Herbeveaux. The pay was $48 a week for four nights' work. It seemed princely to him. Later on, he joined Arnold Johnson's orchestra at a night club called Green Mill Gardens. Two of the girls who were ponies in the Green Mill chorus line were Ruth Etting and Helen Morgan, both of whom were to become gloriously successful singing stars before long.

When he was fifteen, Benny moved over to Art Kassel's 'Kassel in the Air' orchestra at the Midway Gardens, a large and popular ballroom across from Washington Park. It was a step up for him, because the band included some fine jazz men. Besides, Kassel raised no objections to Benny's habit of lying back in his chair on occasion, like Leon Rappolo, and blowing hot. Word got around that Benny was worth listening to, and every now and then a musician from some other orchestra would drop by to hear him play. One evening, the alto sax man Gil Rodin came in. When the band packed up for the night, Gil invited Benny to accompany him on the rounds of a few jazz spots which they both knew. It seemed that Gil was recruiting a number of new players for Ben Pollack's orchestra, out on the West Coast. But it was not until morning that Gil asked if Benny would like to join Pollack's outfit. With no hesitation at all, Benny said he would.

Shortly before his sixteenth birthday, Benny packed a cardboard suitcase and bought his train ticket for California. It was the first time he had gone far from home and the trip took two days. At the far end of the line, Pollack himself met the train and drove Benny straight on to Venice, where the band was working at the time. The ballroom was out on a pier, surrounded by hot-dog stands, roller coasters, and so on. When Benny saw it he said that it looked just like Riverview Park back home in Chicago. Immediately he found himself plunged into rehearsal and loving that part of things. Pollack's band had a free and easy quality which brought to mind such outfits as the Original Dixieland Jazz Band, the Memphis Five and the new Orleans Rhythm Kings. Here, however, the music was more carefully contrived, with punch in the arranged trios for brass and atmosphere in the reed shadings back of solo choruses. Pollack gave his best players plenty of freedom to improvise; but at the same time he achieved overall discipline.

Part of the secret lay in Pollack's arrangements, which were provided by Fud Livingston and a newcomer named Glenn Miller. Taking a hint from black bands such as King Oliver's and Fletcher Henderson's, Fud and Glenn left room for jazz improvisations in the structure of every number. This was a new departure for a sizable white orchestra. It succeeded because it gave the musicians themselves so much more enjoyment — and because they were all gifted instrumentalists. Pollack himself on drums, Glenn Miller on trombone, Fud Livingston as all-round reed man, Gil Rodin on alto sax, Harry Greenberg and Al Harris on cornet, Dick Morgan on banjo, Wayne Allen on piano, and now Benny himself, made up the group. To sit and swing in such fast company for the first time at the age of sixteen, was indeed a thrill.

Customarily, Benny sat next to Pollack's drums. On certain tunes 'the two Bennies' would improvise a dozen or more choruses together. If there were someone in the audience whom Pollack wanted to impress on a particular evening, he would lean across and whisper: 'Make it a million notes a minute, kid, in the low register; give it the personality this time around.'

When the Venice engagement came to an end, Pollack brought the band back home to Chicago, but at first bookings proved hard to find. To strengthen his rhythm section, Pollack took on Benny's brother Harry as tuba and string bass. Then came a break, a long-term engagement at the Southmoor Hotel. Benny, Harry, and some of the older Goodman children were doing well enough by now to enable their father to retire from sweatshop work. In any case the old man's eyes were failing. But he would not retire; self-reliance was still very much part of his American dream. And yet, David Goodman confessed, there was one thing for which he had always wished. That was a chance to work out of doors, in the open air. So finally he obtained a newsstand concession at the corner of California and Madison Avenue. It pleased him to hand out newspapers and count pennies, red-fingered, in the cold wind. He also promised that he would go over one evening to hear Harry and Benny do their stuff at the swank Southmoor. He guessed his only suit was too shabby for such a place as that, but he would be buying a new one soon and then he'd go.

But that was not his destiny. One evening, at about seven o'clock, as David Goodman was leaving the stand to go home and have supper with the youngest children, a speeding car jumped the curb and killed him. He died without a murmur of complaint, as he had lived.

After the Southmoor, Pollack's band was booked into a gangster hangout, the Rendezvous Café, which was ruled by Vince Druse. Vince had a one-chair barbershop installed at the rear of the joint so that his troops could get shaves and hot-towel treatments in peace, without exposing themselves to the razors or bullets of rival baronies. Although the Rendezvous lacked class, it was a pleasant place to work. The mobsters were more thoughtful than most society hosts, regularly cozening Pollack's boys with food and booze on the house.

Having so much steady work made Benny feel rich. He made his first big purchase of a personal sort: a high, wide and handsome black convertible. The car had a tonneau windshield in back of the driver's seat. At speed and especially at night, that windshield looked like a sling for automatic weapons – something with which certain police patrol cars were equipped. Benny enjoyed seeing cops on the beat stiffen to attention as he whizzed by them.

After a long engagement at the Rendezvous came another step up to one of the best-known places in the Loop: the Blackhawk Restaurant. The Blackhawk catered to a collegiate crowd, the raccoon-coat set. Mobsters referred to such young clientele, in tones of mingled wistfulness and scorn, as 'Indians'. Firewater in silver hip-flasks was part of their savage accoutrement. In the late 1920s many young people had money to spend, nightlife flourished, and musicians did well enough. Even the 'Wild West Side Mob' of Benny's schoolboy pals were starting to succeed professionally. Frank Teschemacher, Davey Tough, Bud Freeman, Jimmy McPartland and some others had their own band – the Wolverines – which played most nights at a South Side amusement park called White City. By contrast with the busy, blurry, boozed-up exuberance of the Wolverines, Pollack's band sounded virtually conservative. Ben took steps to correct that impression by raiding the Wolverines to recruit Jimmy McPartland's hot cornet.

Joe Sullivan, Milt Mezzrow, Eddie Condon and others of a jazz-mad crowd were to be found at a dive called the Three Deuces to indicate its address: 222 State Street. Downstairs at the Deuces, in a dismal unpainted room reeking of gin, the boys would sometimes jam until dawn or beyond. On one of the nights when Benny and Ben Pollack sat in there together, they built chorus after chorus of *I Want To Be Happy* with clarinet and drums alone. Looking back now, Benny sees it as a sort of dry run for what he was to do with Gene Krupa years later on *Sing, Sing, Sing*.

The Wild West Side Mob and Pollack's relatively smooth stable of jazz instrumentalists were prone to disagree on what constituted the best music. All the same they tremendously enjoyed jamming together, and the Three Deuces was their common ground.

When an old pal from out of town, Bix Beiderbecke, turned up one night, Benny and some of the others swept him off to the Sunset Club to hear Louis Armstrong and Earl Hines. From there they went to an upstairs joint called The Nest, and jammed into the daylight hours with Jimmy Noone. Over breakfast, Bix mentioned the fact that he had to catch a train back to Detroit and play in Jean

Goldkette's orchestra that night. The whole gang decided to go along and piled into the train with Bix.

By early afternoon they were ensconced in his Detroit hotel room, listening to records and sipping gin. When darkness came, they trailed raggedly over to the Greystone Ballroom where the Goldkette band was playing. Refused admission at the front entrance, they managed to get in at the stage door. Along with Bix, the band boasted such musicians as Joe Venuti and Frankie Trumbauer. It was all worth hearing, though by then the Chicago contingent considered it less of a lark than they had the night before.

At the start of 1928 Pollack made his big move, this time to New York. The band had been booked into the Little Club in the basement of the 44th Street Theater just west of Broadway. It proved a success there from the beginning. The club featured a floor show with Lillian Roth, and this helped to pull in customers. Sunday night was an occasion for jam sessions, when musicians from other bands dropped by. Miff Mole, Eddie Lang, Red Nichols and Jack Teagarden sat in often.

After the Little Club, Pollack's band had a number of engagements before settling in at New York's Park Central Hotel. Soon after their arrival, the gangster Arnold Rothstein was shot on the premises. Collegiates took to calling the place 'the Shooting Gallery', and swarmed in. Among the steady customers were a pair of songwriters, Dorothy Fields and Jimmy McHugh, who were collaborating on a show called *Hello Daddy*, which was to star Dorothy's father, Lew Fields. They asked Pollack if he would consider putting his band in the pit for the show. Fortunately this turned out to be a highly successful experiment.

These were happy-go-lucky times, when Benny made a habit of rooming with or near his brother Harry, Gil Rodin, Jimmy McPartland and, until Glenn left the gang to get married and pursue his own career, with Miller as well. However, relations between the two Bennies were beginning to deteriorate. One problem was that Ben Pollack could not entirely approve of Benny's new custom of recruiting members from the Pollack Orchestra to cut free-lance records for small companies such as Banner, Oriole and Melotone. The sides they made ranged from an occasional diamond of improvisation down to sheer corn. Embarrassingly enough, the worst examples, such as *Shirt Tail Stomp*, sold by far the best. The public appeared to prefer musical high-jinks to jazz with real emotion in it. Nevertheless, most of the records which the constantly shifting group managed to produce had a certain degree of guts. Benny Goodman's Boys, Ten Freshmen, Lumberjacks, Dixie Daisies, Cotton Pickers, Kentucky Grasshoppers, Southern Nighthawks, the Hotsy Totsy Gang, and The Whoopee Makers – such were the names chosen for the record labels.

The nucleus of The Whoopee Makers was the Goodman brothers, Gil Rodin, Jimmy McPartland, and finally the man who had taken Glenn Miller's chair in the Pollack outfit: Jack Teagarden. Old friends who had come east from Chicago – Bud Freeman, Davey Tough and Joe Sullivan among them – sat in from time to time. So did such lions of the New York jazz scene as Wingy Manone, Joe Venuti, Eddie Lang, and Tommy and Jimmy Dorsey. These men, and dozens more like them, were often bored with dance-band or pit-band playing. To jam for money, on the contrary, was an ideal situation – not that monetary rewards were great, as yet, in the record industry.

**T**wenty when he finally broke with Ben Pollack, Benny felt he had reached the point where independence was necessary for him. Besides, although the public knew little about him as yet, fellow musicians were admiring. It seemed likely that odd jobs with pick-up bands and in recording studios would come his way. As things developed he did find work, but not nearly so often as he would have liked. His first useful breaks as an independent were thanks to a Dixieland-style cornet player and jazz entrepreneur whose name was Red Nichols. Red's 'Five Pennies' was a band which formed and dissolved again as the occasion might warrant. Although billed as a five-man team for the sake of the pun on Nichols' name, it generally ran to eight or nine. Benny was often one of them, both at the Hollywood Restaurant on Broadway and at recording sessions. Among the classic sides the Pennies cut with Benny in their midst were *Chinatown, On The Alamo, Dinah,* and *Indiana* – all four distinguished by the ebullient drumming of a young man fresh off the train from Chicago: Gene Krupa.

Along with Benny and his brother Harry, Gene also contributed to an all-star recording session which was led by the gentle song-writer Hoagy Carmichael. The others involved were Bubber Miley, Bud Freeman, Irv Brodsky, Eddie Lang, Tommy and Jimmy Dorsey, and significantly, Bix Beiderbecke. Together they did an historic job on *Rockin' Chair.* They also brought off a rollicking performance of *Barnacle Bill The Sailor* which reminded Benny of boyhood days when he'd been part of the old Hull House band, jamming out in the woods in short pants after a church picnic.

Not long after this, Bix Beiderbecke himself organized a session to cut *I'll Be A Friend 'With Pleasure', I Don't Mind Walkin' In The Rain,* and *Deep Down South* for Victor. On this date there were no fewer than three hot clarinets: Pee Wee Russell, Jimmy Dorsey and Benny. It wasn't that Bix really needed all three, but he was the sort of person who could not bring himself to leave any close friends out of a deal.

In 1930 and 1931, Benny was mainly freelancing, trying to make his living entirely by means of recording sessions. Among those with whom he recorded was Ted Lewis, the same musician he had extravagantly admired and imitated as a child; an inferior instrumentalist, to be sure, but an ineffable showman. One of those recording dates (6 March 1931) produced a truly classic pair of sides. Ted had lined up not only Benny, but the jubilant tenor sax man from

Chicago, Bud Freeman. Better still, he had invited Fats Waller to play piano and sing. *Dallas Blues* and *Royal Garden Blues* made up the perfect program for Waller. In the midst of an ecstatic Waller solo, Ted leaned across and demanded aloud in his time-honored but schmaltzy manner: 'Is everybody happy?' Fats did not take offence at the intervention, because in fact he *was* happy; and so they all were at that moment.

But in general these were not happy days. Benny had brought his mother and younger brothers east from Chicago and installed them in a Jackson Heights apartment. He would go out there for Sunday lunches, but there never seemed to be much to talk about on these occasions. At the same time he was sharing bachelor digs in midtown Manhattan with a Yale dropout and playboy named 'Whiskey' Smith. They did a good deal of partying, but not often with the hot musicians Benny was most at home with. He felt that he was burdened with new responsibilities, empty pleasures, and frequent joblessness.

Occasional breaks there were, but these seldom turned out exactly as expected. Once, for instance, Benny received a flattering offer to assemble a band of his own for a one-night stand at a Williams College prom. Among the musicians whom he asked along where Tommy Dorsey and Bix Beiderbecke. Unfortunately, Tommy and Bix were both under the impression that Williams was in the region of New Haven and decided to take the afternoon train there together. By the time they discovered their error, it was too late to go by train at all. In desperation, they did a rare thing for those distant days: they chartered a plane. Thick snow prevented them from landing anywhere near Williams itself, so they covered the last twenty miles by taxicab. Bix had been sick before the trip began, and that night he passed out cold on the stand. According to legend, Benny picked up the cornet which Bix let fall and played the interrupted chorus through. He cannot remember it now, but believes he might have done so. What he does remember is Bix sprawled out like a broken puppet. He had a strong feeling that Bix would burn out entirely within a matter of months and die.

In 1930 and again in 1931, George and Ira Gershwin wrote the songs and lyrics for two musical comedies on Broadway, the first called *Strike Up The Band* and the second *Girl Crazy*. For each of these hits, Red Nichols conducted the pit orchestra and among his pit men were Glenn Miller, Gene Krupa, a fine tenor sax man named Babe Russin and Benny. Gershwin music had a great deal to recommend it, yet Benny was inevitably bored playing precisely the same notes show after show. One night, to relieve the monotony a little, he ornamented his written clarinet part with an assertive vibrato and some comical off-notes.

Red took Benny to task after the performance, and other members of the band who happened to be listening joined in condemning Benny's action. Bewildered and miserable, Benny glared around for a moment or two and then spluttered: 'But I was only kidding!' Turning to Red, he added on a sudden impulse: 'Know how I sound when I'm kidding? Well, that's how you sound all the time!'

Red looked surprised, and let the matter go. Others, however, were less tolerant of Benny's developing temperament. It surprised and nettled him to find that he had a reputation for arrogance. It has never been claimed for Benny that he had the instincts of a diplomat. In those days he tended to be reticent and, when he did speak, unexpectedly negative. On the other hand, Benny was always immensely loyal to relatives and friends, as well as to the musicians whom he wholeheartedly admired. Moreover, he had begun to display a natural flair for leadership. A record cut for Columbia on 9 February 1931, by 'The Charlestown Chasers under the direction of Benny Goodman', made that much very clear indeed.

The first two sides recorded on that date, *When Your Lover Has Gone* and *Walkin' My Baby Back Home*, featured vocals by Paul Small, together with some startlingly tender clarinet choruses. The second pair, *Beale Street Blues* and *Basin Street Blues*, pointed towards the future; besides their obvious quality, they demonstrated a unique, easy sort of swing which would forever afterwards be associated with Benny Goodman's name. To make the set, he had brought together Gene Krupa, his brother Harry, Dick McDonough, Art Schutt, Larry Binyon, Sid Stoneburn, Ruby Weinstein, Charlie and Jack Teagarden, and Glenn Miller. The blues vocals were by Jack Teagarden, and the blues arrangements by Glenn Miller.

Benny's affairs, like those of the nation as a whole, reached a nadir during the early 1930s. His first opportunity to buck the general doldrums of the Depression was offered by Con Conrad, manager of the singer Russ Columbo. It was Conrad's idea that Benny should put together a band to back Russ, who was extremely popular (particularly with the ladies) at that time. With a group that included Gene Krupa, Joe Sullivan and 'Whiskey' Wilson, Benny managed an engagement with some success at the Woodmanston Inn in Westchester.

Then, on a September evening in 1933, a crew-cut ivy-leaguer stepped up to him in the old Onyx Club on 52nd Street, and introduced himself as John Hammond. Hammond explained that he'd been requested to produce a number of hot records for sale in Europe, and he wanted to know if Benny would be interested. At first Benny thought not; the deal appeared to hold out little if any profit.

But the two young men fell into conversation, and before long Benny was won round. Krupa, Teagarden and Joe Sullivan were among the musicians immediately decided upon. For too long, such vastly talented members of the old crowd had been scrambling for jobs on their own. Hammond and Benny agreed that this chance to play together again would mean more than money to each man.

**B**oth Teagarden and Krupa were at the time in New England, playing in Mal Hallett's orchestra. They gladly came down to New York for the first recording session which took place on 18 October 1933. Others on the date, besides Joe Sullivan and Benny, were the guitarist Dick McDonough, Art Bernstein on bass, Art Karle as second trombone, and Charlie Teagarden and Mannie Klein on trumpets. *I Gotta Right To Sing The Blues* and *Ain'tcha Glad?*, both arranged by Art Schutt, were the sides they cut. The vocals by Big T, as Jack Teagarden was called, with their high emotional voltage in his deceptively languid style of delivery, helped to put both numbers across. The sides were afterwards pirated by a brash record-buccaneer under the 'Jolly Roger' label, whose candor amused Benny.

Before their second session, on 27 October, Joe Sullivan took off for California. Frank Froeba came in to replace Joe on piano, but the group was otherwise the same as before. They began with a new composition by McDonough called *Dr. Heckle And Mr. Jibe*. Then came *Texas Tea Party*, which Benny and Big T had dreamed up together, the title referring to Teagarden's name and place of birth, and also to marijuana.

The results of these efforts were universally pleasing. Ben Selvin at Columbia Records decided to release the first two sides in the United States, where they sold surprisingly well. At the Commodore

Music Shop on 42nd Street, Milt Gabler exhibited the disk together with a card listing every musician on it. This was something absolutely new in record promotion, and it set an important precedent.

During the next few months, John Hammond helped to enlarge Benny's circle of jazz colleagues. Together they toured Harlem nightspots where Hammond arranged introductions and worked out agreements to make records. Billie Holiday and Bessie Smith were among the stars of the shifting and deepening jazz firmament in which Benny now found himself. It was in this period that he worked briefly with both of them, and with many a lesser light from north of 110th Street. One date that he remembers with special gratification is 2 February 1934; that was when Benny recorded four sides with a brilliantly talented singer, Mildred Bailey, doing the vocals. The tenor sax on that date was a titan of the Harlem jazz scene: Coleman Hawkins. The numbers they performed together were *Georgia Jubilee, Junk Man, Ol' Pappy* and *Emaline*.

At the beginning of 1934 Benny was living with his mother and younger brothers in Jackson Heights, and was earning on average no more than $40 a week. In March, Ben Pollack's band returned to New York from a long cross-country tour and settled in at Billy Rose's Casino de Paree on 54th Street. Harry Goodman, who was still with Pollack, moved in at Jackson Heights and brought exciting news. It appeared that Billy Rose was planning to open a second club, a theater-restaurant to be known as 'Billy Rose's Music Hall'. He would need an orchestra, and Harry, along with a mutual friend named Oscar Levant, urged Benny to try to fill that spot. Benny would certainly be set if he could put together a band and, in effect, sell it to Billy Rose.

Here was a fork in the road. Jack Teagarden had recently accepted a comfortable berth in the prosperous band led by Paul Whiteman. Paul had offered Benny a similar deal, a long-term contract calling for a great many one-night stands out of town. Benny could not decide whether to accept the Whiteman proposal or to follow the advice of his brother and Oscar Levant. In the end he chose the more difficult and potentially rewarding path of recruiting a band of his own; and from then on he was to accept the full responsibilities of leadership in music.

His first requirement was a strong rhythm section: bass, guitar, piano and drums. Then he needed three trumpets, two trombones and three saxophones. He would in fact have preferred four saxophones, but that was one more than he thought he could afford. Besides, his own clarinet would considerably strengthen the reed section. The instrumentalists Benny would have chosen first of all were mostly under contract to other bands, and he was in no position to outbid them. Even so, he managed to pick up an outstanding group, chiefly by promising each man the freedom to play hot and to solo a good deal if he wanted to. Added to that, he provided firm leadership, especially in rehearsals. Benny believed that blend of tone and uniform phrasing were a prime necessity, and fortunately the musicians whom he had gathered agreed with that philosophy. A steady few among them – Art Rollini, Hymie Schertzer and Red Ballard in particular – were to remain with him for years thereafter.

The venture began propitiously. Billy Rose auditioned the band, and after a week or so, signed it on for a long stay at his new Music Hall. This promised an important and very welcome change in Benny's way of life and that of the men who would be playing with him. With rare exceptions they had been leading a catch-as-catch-can professional existence, with no security, no continuity, no chances to pick and choose. Now they were to be together night after night – an authentic orchestra. But it turned out to be a tough and unhappy engagement, one that Benny has called 'distraught'. The band were meant to play for the elaborate floor show as well as for dancing; but soon after starting they were told that they would be restricted to the latter and another band would take over the show responsibility. Still, they played seriously and well for the dancing, and gradually became a tight and well-exercised group, with such outstanding musicians among their ranks as Claude Thornhill on the piano and George van Epps on guitar. One night Benny stood back and listened to them, and said to himself, 'This really isn't a bad band!' And then suddenly, after three months, they were given notice, along with Billy Rose himself.

This was a devastating blow, for Benny could not possibly carry the full band's salaries without steady work. At the moment when it looked as if he would have to quit bandleading as a regular thing, a well-timed break occurred in his fortunes.

At that time radio was as ubiquitous and commercial a force as any in America. The networks held the population, like million-eared fish, in thrall. To be part of a regular sponsored program on a coast-to-coast network was a major ambition of anyone in the entertainment business. Therefore, when the National Biscuit Company proposed establishing a weekly three-hour music show on NBC on Saturday nights – from 10 p.m. to 1 a.m. on the East Coast, and then with a two-hour repeat for the West Coast – every bandleader was ready to compete for a part in the deal. Fifty-three radio stations across the country were involved and the program envisioned three permanent bands – a sweet one, a rhumba one, and finally a hot one – to play alternate sets.

Benny had been doing some sporadic radio work set up for him by Joe Bonime, of an advertising agency in New York. When the National Biscuit Company announcement was made, Bonime thought Benny ought at least to try for the hot band spot, and arranged what Benny calls 'an audition for an audition'. Bonime came along to hear what Benny's boys could do and was so impressed that he advised without hesitation that they should offer themselves for a hearing. The unexpected and electrifying result was that Benny's band was selected and given the contract.

**B**enny was stunned when he received the news by phone. It may have been the single most important break in his life. It meant that the men would be earning around $125 for a single night's work – what they had been getting for a week. He remembers now that the first thought which came to him was that from then on everything would be different. A door to personal glory had inched open, and he had slipped in. He did not doubt that there would be setbacks ahead, and plenty of them; but fame and fortune would also be part of the mixture.

Benny cannot recall exactly when the notion of forming a jazz trio first occurred to him, but he believes the seeds may have been sown one evening at a party given by Red Norvo and his wife Mildred Bailey. Among insiders at least, the Norvos were possibly the most admired couple in the whole jazz world. Red played xylophone in an extraordinarily imaginative and understated style, letting the notes drift by like ghosts cloaked in their separate silences; and Mildred was a highly respected song stylist. At that particular party, the guests had all been musicians too. But just one man among them had the courage to sit down at the piano and entertain, launching into a cool series of variations on *Body And Soul*. Clean, endlessly fecund, flawless – Teddy Wilson's playing was all those things and more. Benny was so moved by this music that he unpacked his clarinet, and in the low register floated some ideas of his own upon the rhythmic figures which flowed steadily from Teddy's iron-firm left hand. What they produced might be called jazz in the manner of chamber music.

Soon after that night, he brought Teddy together with his own favorite drummer, Gene Krupa, and they made the first Trio recordings for Victor on 13 July 1935. The four sides cut on that date were *Someday, Sweetheart*; *Who?*; *After You've Gone*; and *Body And Soul*.

The conventions of the period called for dance bands to be either all-white or all-black, with no exceptions. The color barrier mocked and marred the whole spirit of jazz; but not even in those days did anyone object to black and white musicians joining forces at private parties, late-night jam sessions, or in recording studios. So Teddy had no difficulty in crossing the barrier to record with Benny and Gene. For his part, Benny crossed it in the other direction when he sat in with a group assembled by Teddy to record with Billie Holiday. *What A Little Moonlight Can Do*, *I Wished On The Moon*, and *Miss Brown To You* were the songs from that session in 1935 and the brilliant instrumental group Teddy brought together for the occasion included Roy Eldridge on trumpet, Ben Webster on tenor sax, John Trueheart on guitar, John Kirby on string bass, and Cozy Cole on drums.

**I**n those days (and indeed for a good many years afterwards) Benny's own orchestra relied on the behind-the-scenes genius of gentle Fletcher Henderson. 'Smack', as Henderson's friends called him, was a much-loved bandleader of rich experience, a fine jazz pianist, and finally a creative arranger in a class by himself. His orchestrations were quite unlike the tricky and elaborate work of better-known arrangers such as Paul Whiteman's Ferde Grofe. Smack wrote more directly from the heart, in a style that inspired relaxed musicianship. His brass ensembles had both bark and bite; his reeds could whisper sweetly, or roll up a gale. By alternating reeds and brasses against the varied but unremitting beat of the rhythm section – drums, bass, piano and guitar – he created dialogues in music.

**B**enny still feels that one of Smack's most memorable arrangements was of *Blue Skies*. It turned Irving Berlin's neat melody into a spacious and exhilarating experience. Yet when he first saw the Henderson score, Benny found it puzzling. It started with a rough-edged and heavily punctuated introduction, which didn't seem to fit with what came later on. Respectfully, he asked Smack to comment on that aspect. 'Don't you see?', Smack replied softly, with a melancholy smile. 'There has to be some stormy weather before the blue skies begin to appear!'

In the same months when the Goodman Trio was first launching its historic association and recordings were being made with Billie Holiday, the full Benny Goodman orchestra was also producing classic renditions of Smack's arrangements. *Sometimes I'm Happy* was one; *Between The Devil And The Deep Blue Sea*, with a stunning vocal by Helen Ward, was another. Bunny Berigan had just joined the band; his big warm trumpet tones and the sweetness of his inspiration did much to put across *King Porter* and *Blue Skies*. Sides such as these amounted to a tremendous breakthrough for Benny personally and for the band as a whole. They matched anything that the leading hot orchestras of the age – Duke Ellington's, Chick Webb's, and Jimmy Lunceford's – could accomplish. Never before had a white band entered such exalted lists of musical combat, or been honored for it. At the end of that year, to Benny's intense delight, the authoritative jazz journal *Metronome* rated his 'The best swing band of 1935'.

At the time of this recognition, Benny's orchestra had settled into Chicago for a long engagement at the Congress Hotel. Smack Henderson came out to Chicago soon afterwards with a brand-new band of his own to play at the Grand Terrace. After work, on some nights, members of both orchestras would get together for jam sessions at the Di Lisa Club, on the South Side. Chu Berry and Roy Eldridge from Smack's organization, plus Gene Krupa and Benny himself, seemed to enjoy those occasions together most.

A number of jazz enthusiasts in the Chicago area had organized themselves into The Rhythm Club, headed by an energetic cosmopolite named Helen Oakley. She had formed it in imitation of the 'Hot Clubs' already prevalent in Europe, and members held meetings to play and discuss particular jazz records, as well as to give moral support to bands which they liked. Helen Oakley, however, had bigger plans. With some difficulty, she persuaded Benny to present a jazz concert one Sunday afternoon in the Urban Room of the Congress Hotel. To everyone's astonishment, it was a sell-out and a smash success. The magazine *Down Beat* described the performance as 'the warmest swing session in the memory of Joe Public . . . a landmark in swing history.'

Thanks to an editor of *Time* magazine, Frank Norris, the concert received national publicity, and Benny's fame was given a boost. The Rhythm Club soon followed the Goodman concert with one featuring Fletcher Henderson. Smack fielded a superb group, including not only Chu Berry and Roy Eldridge but also bass player John Kirby and the titanically driving drummer Big Sid Catlett. In years to come, as it turned out, trumpeter Eldridge was to star in an orchestra led by Gene Krupa, while for a few months in 1941 Catlett was to occupy Gene's old throne in Benny's band.

The Rhythm Club's final concert of 1936 was held on Easter Sunday. Benny's band appeared once again, and with it, the Goodman Trio. Teddy Wilson, who was playing at that time at the 'Famous Door' night club in New York, came out to Chicago for the weekend, riding the New York Central sleeper *Twentieth Century*, to complete the group. There was psychological pressure on Teddy for it was the first time a black musician would be appearing in public with a white group. Luckily, grace under pressure is a personal characteristic of Teddy's. He rose to the occasion, dissolving the so-called color barrier with nothing but handfuls of delicate sound.

After the show, Benny asked Teddy if he would consider joining the Goodman organization on a permanent basis. Teddy said that he would not only consider it, he would *do* it. At that moment, an important new precedent was set: not just within Benny's group but also for jazz in general.

During the summer, Benny brought his organization out to Hollywood in order to participate in a bizarre musical-comedy movie – *The Big Broadcast Of 1937* – which also starred Jack Benny, Martha Raye and Leopold Stokowski, among others. That potpourri of effort marked the start of a long, although intermittent, affair between Benny and Hollywood – one which added zest to a number of films. The relationship was to reach its climax in a well-meant but marshmallow embrace in 1956, when Hollywood released its film tribute entitled *The Benny Goodman Story*.

Halfway through the shooting of *Big Broadcast*, Benny received a cryptic message from John Hammond in New York. It urged him to visit a seedy sailors' dive in downtown Los Angeles which was known as 'The Paradise Cafe'. Benny took this advice and visited the cafe, paying an entrance charge of one dime. Inside, the master of ceremonies, bandleader and star performer all turned out to be one man: Lionel Hampton, with his vibraphone. Benny listened and watched. For hour after hour, Hampton had the harsh, dreary little place overflowing with gaiety. The next evening Benny was back again, this time with Gene Krupa and Teddy Wilson. After midnight, when the last sailor and prostitute had vanished into outer darkness, Lionel locked the door on the inside and invited his new friends to jam with him. They began, Benny remembers, with *Dinah*. As each man in turn created chorus after chorus on the theme, the stale-smelling dimness of the Paradise lit up in mutual joy. Teddy, Gene, Benny, and now Lionel, seemed to play together just as naturally as the fingers of a single hand.

Lionel was a religious man who never travelled without his Bible. He once told Benny he believed that God had not been far away the first time they joined forces. Benny himself was not religious in the least – unless music could be called a religion – but he had no difficulty understanding what Lionel meant to express. Not many days later, on 21 August 1936, the Goodman Quartet recorded its first number: *Moon Glow*. Then on 26 August, they pressed *Dinah*, *Exactly Like You*, and a spontaneous composition of their own devising which they called *Vibraphone Blues*. Lionel had by now agreed to join the Goodman organization as soon as he finished his contract at the Paradise.

Since his early training had been quite solid, Benny knew the classical clarinet repertory even though he concentrated on jazz. At one time or other he had studied or listened to the masterpieces of clarinet music: Mozart's *Quintet*, *Trio* and *Concerto*, Weber's two *Concerti* and his *Concertino*, Brahms's *Quintet*, *Sonata* and *Trio*. His career as a classical artist was to be established some years later, but one of his first public performances in this field was at a musicale in the ballroom of John Hammond's mother's private house on East 91st Street. John had been practising the viola part of Mozart's *Quintet For Clarinet And Strings In A-Major* with a chamber music group and invited Benny to join in. After some weeks of intermittent rehearsal, they had the piece under fair control, and on a May evening they performed it for a number of invited guests. Benny felt nervous enough to accept a couple of sidecars in the hour before they were to play. But the performance went well, and the only dissonance Benny can remember is that one of the gilt chairs on which the guests were sitting broke during the course of the evening.

**T**his new direction in the application of his prodigious talent did not detract Benny from his dedication to jazz. If anything, it added resonance to his appreciation of the jazz medium. It seemed appropriate, somehow, that Mrs. Hammond's musical evening closed with some spectacular blues singing by Mildred Bailey, brilliantly accompanied by Fletcher Henderson on piano.

In 1947, together with his friend the violinist, Joseph Szigeti, Benny commissioned Bela Bartók to write a piece called *Contrasts For Clarinet, Violin And Piano*. He was also to enlarge the repertoire by commissioning other modern classical works which he played with the leading orchestras of the world. Among his happiest recollections of classical performances was one he gave at Memorial Hall, Cambridge, in the spring of 1964. On this occasion his daughter Rachel was the pianist and together they performed Brahms's *Sonata*, Weber's *Grand Duo Concertino*, and Bohuslav Martinu's *Sonatina*. He also treasures an earlier memory of the evening he joined with Yehudi Menuhin and Leon Powers to play Darius Milhaud's *Suite For Clarinet, Violin and Piano*.

There were also some noble experiments in that uncertain area between 'legitimate' music and jazz. For example, he has recorded Stravinsky's *Ebony Concerto*, Morton Gould's *Derivations For Clarinet And Band*, and Leonard Bernstein's *Prelude, Fugue, And Riffs*, under each composer's own baton. While these are occasions that he likes to recall, they probably seem relatively unimportant to his public at large. Benny realizes that most people have always thought of him first and last as a jazz clarinetist and bandleader. As 'King of Swing', a soubriquet which has stuck with him from the great era around 1936, his contributions to music have been in the vernacular. And even there he had a long struggle to endure before the popular crown descended, so to speak, upon his head.

One-night stands, for instance: those had been the bane of his existence when the Goodman band was new. He had no choice at that time but to take his orchestra far and wide. Bookings were scarce and mostly out of town, despite the best efforts of his new agent, Willard Alexander of the Music Corporation of America (MCA). Alexander was a college graduate, Benny's own age, who appreciated hot music. He held the view that there were many college kids who felt the same way about jazz and he believed that collegiate backing was something on which Benny could build. Alexander was fresh and young, working for an agency which was expanding and open to new ventures. Benny and Alexander liked each other from the start; to their mutual profit, they joined forces in a business way.

Benny's opportunity to get off the treadmill of long tours and one-night stands was the result of an unexpectedly successful and by now famous engagement in Los Angeles. This was back in the late summer of 1935, not long after the band had actually been established and engaged in a spate of Victor recording sessions. The tour through parts of the Midwest and the Rockies area aroused very faint and few cheers; a stand at Elitch's Gardens in Denver, Colorado, had been particularly discouraging. So it was not surprising that MCA should consider cancelling the last engagements on the Coast.

Willard Alexander, however, blocked this drastic decision. He felt that, after the hardships of a cross-country tour and especially one with disappointing audiences, the band at least deserved a West Coast hearing. So the final engagement of the trip, a full month at the prestigious Palomar Ballroom in Los Angeles, was tentatively allowed to stand. A few weeks before that appearance the band played a Monday night at a ballroom in Oakland called McFaddens, with a capacity of 1500. The band's exposure on the Saturday night 'Let's Dance' program throughout the year had given it sufficient renown to draw about a thousand enthusiasts to this second-rate upstairs dancery, who howled with near-fanatical delight.

The Palomar, at the corner of Vermont and Third Avenue in downtown Los Angeles, was an infinitely tougher and more important hurdle. It had a large restaurant section and a huge dance floor. Admission was no more than half a dollar, and whether for that reason or because young Californians were curious to hear the Goodman orchestra, a sizable crowd turned out on opening night.

For the first hour, Benny played it safe. He called for the sweetest, softest, most gently and dreamily danceable arrangements in the band's books. The response was polite and no more. Then suddenly Benny felt something snap, as it were, inside his soul. For all he knew, this might be the band's last night together. He decided they should ride it out in their own way, and this one last time fully enjoy themselves.

Accordingly, at the start of the next set, he offered one of the band's own favorites: a Fletcher Henderson arrangement. Which one it was precisely, he cannot now recall; but the great roar of recognition which went up from the crowd was possibly the sweetest sound Benny had ever heard. It was obvious that the kids had all been waiting for the band to really swing, along the lines that had first excited them via radio and records. More than half the people on the floor stopped dancing and came surging up around the orchestra. They clustered, ten or fifteen thick on three sides of the stand, like a dense bank of reeds, letting the music wash across and through them, and swaying just a little.

Jack Teagarden once remarked that it was great to see people dancing, because you knew they were happy. Benny agrees with that comment. Yet happier still, it seems to him, was that listening stillness in the Palomar Ballroom. Each man in the band rose joyously to the occasion and played better than at any time since leaving New York. *When Buddha Smiles, Down South Camp Meeting* never sounded as exciting as on that night.

MCA's West Coast headquarters were delighted to have been proven wrong about Benny. They were only recently established on the West Coast, and this success gave them a welcome boost. The office shot off a grateful telegram to Willard Alexander in New York to announce that it had been a sensational opening. The Palomar management, for its part, doubled Benny's booking from one month to two. During this engagement, every local attendance record was to fall.

Benny and the entire band now found themselves elevated to a dizzying high-wire of popular acclaim. That high-wire was to stretch right on through the remainder of the 1930s into the mists and dislocations of World War II. To walk up there, while the tumultuous applause of thousands upon thousands of people welled up all around you, was gratifying and yet rather frightening as well.

**I**n March 1937, at the Paramount Theater in New York, the growing adulation reached its first remarkable climax. At this period Benny's band was playing the Madhattan Room of the Hotel Pennsylvania, which had become the most popular music room in New York with the college trade. The Paramount Theater booking doubled the band's workload; but the money they could earn from it would be nice to have. Benny himself had no idea that the job would be other than routine. For one thing, movie theater audiences in the past had not proved particularly responsive to swing. For another, the film constituting the other half of the Paramount's bill was a rather somber affair about witchcraft in New England, starring Claudette Colbert and Fred MacMurray, called *Maid Of Salem*. As a *New Yorker* profile, published shortly after the event, put it, 'For months there had been dance bands at the Paramount, among them such impressive organizations as Fred Waring's and Ray Noble's, and the theater had no reason to expect that Benny Goodman's fourteen-piece swing outfit was going to start the patrons dancing in the aisles. That's just what it did, though.' On the first morning, when Benny and the band arrived at the theater for 7 a.m. rehearsals, they found a line already at the box-office and stretching all round the block. It dawned on Benny, not then but soon afterwards, that there might be thousands of brand-new Goodman fans who were not in the night-club league; kids who could, however, scrape together thirty-five cents for a theater ticket. According to the *New Yorker*'s statistics, there were 4,400 people on the line at 10 a.m. waiting for the theater to open.

After rehearsals, the orchestra assembled nervously in the sunken pit of the theater. The morning show, the first of five which they were scheduled to play that day and every day for two weeks, was about to start. Machinery whirred, and the band was gently lifted up, as on the palm of some mechanical giant's hand, into the presence of the audience. The band could see at a glance that the house was packed solid. Rank upon rank of young admirers stamped their feet and whistled in welcome.

While being hoisted into view, the band offered the strains of *Let's Dance*, now becoming familiar as Benny Goodman's signature tune. Without a break, it launched from that into *Bugle Call Rag*. Later came *Ridin' High*, by which time kids were shagging and bobbing in the aisles.

When the pandemonium became too much, Benny sat down and just waited. His attitude said: 'When you're through with your concert, we'll get on with ours.' Finally the clamor abated sufficiently for the Quartet to weigh in with *Body And Soul*. The full band played *Tiger Rag*, then *I Got Rhythm* and finally *Sing, Sing, Sing*. Each number seemed to be stepping up the pressure: Gene Krupa tomtomming, raging, grinning, tangle-haired: Vido Musso bellowing and bawling on the tenor sax: Harry James giving out lightning flashes of fanfare, up, through, and around the beat.

**F**ive times a day, held over for three weeks, this unprecedented show was put on, attendance topping twenty-one thousand day after day. *Variety*, the trade paper of the entertainment industry, called the reception 'tradition-shattering in its spontaneity, its unanimity, its sincerity, its volume.'

This was total success; and after this acclaim Benny's life was never the same. His annual income was reported in 1937 to be around a hundred thousand dollars. But the most revolutionary concert of his whole career was the one which took place on the evening of 16 January 1938 at Carnegie Hall in New York. The fame of that event, however, did not spread far until some dozen years later. Fortunately, the whole of it was on record. Albert Marx, the husband of vocalist Helen Ward, had seen to that, using a single overhead mike. The LPs which were first produced in 1950 from Marx's sound document marked a turning point not only in the history of jazz but in that of the record industry also. They rank among the best-selling jazz albums ever produced.

But as Benny stood nervously, complete with blue carnation, on the stage of Carnegie Hall on the night itself, a cold Sunday, he nearly hated the publicist Wynn Nathanson for having thought up the idea of his appearance there, as well as shrewd Sol Hurok for putting his name to it. Hurok has written that Benny must make sure that his boys showed proper 'decorum'. Carnegie Hall was the regular home of conductor John Barbirolli and the New York Philharmonic Orchestra; and tonight it was going to have to jump with hot jazz, or be witness to a dismal failure. If Benny's band flopped he would be blamed – and rightly – for having put it in an impossible position. That was especially true of those black friends, each man a jazz star, whom Benny had persuaded to take part in the concert. It was perhaps understandable, in the circumstances, that he set the beat for the first number too slow. Edgar Sampson's fine composition, *Don't Be That Way*, got off to a lurching start: but luckily, after a tense minute or two, Krupa produced a shatteringly powerful drum solo which jolted the piece back into its correct groove. The audience cheered tumultuously; suddenly everyone seemed to feel that the evening was going to be a free-wheeling bash after all.

Count Basie's *One O'Clock Jump* elicited a tidal wave of applause. Next Benny offered a lighthearted thumbnail history of jazz, including his own imitation of Ted Lewis on clarinet. After that came a graceful tribute to Duke Ellington, by three particularly splendid musicians from Ellington's own band: trumpeter Cootie Williams (who joined the Goodman band in 1940), Johnny Hodges on alto sax, and shy Harry Carney half-hidden behind his melodious baritone saxophone.

Benny's own band returned to the stage in a blasting rendition of *Life Goes To A Party*. The Goodman Trio and Quartet came next, followed by Martha Tilton's show-stopping song: *Loch Lomond*. Jimmy Mundy's *Swingtime In The Rockies* inspired Ziggy Elman to a surpassingly brilliant trumpet flight. And finally, when it appeared as if the evening's terrific pace must have exhausted everyone, Gene began tapping in the beat for the climax: *Sing, Sing, Sing*. He and Benny alone together carried that number on and on, chorus after chorus, ecstatically. Then, as the band came in on the tune again, Jess Stacy, who was relatively unknown at that time, meditatively plinked out some soft church music on piano. Benny gazed round at him in utter astonishment, laughing as he did so, and yells of happiness went sounding through the hall. Many who were there that evening remember Stacy's solo as one of the shining highlights of the whole concert, and Benny thought at the time that Stacy, whom he called 'a sedate kind of player,' was 'stealing the show completely.'

What the Goodman band established in that Carnegie Hall performance was the idea of a jazz concert; until then, orchestras of one type or another had merely provided the music for dancing. The idea of asking people to buy tickets for seats in a concert hall and to provide them with anything but classical music had not occurred before. *Down Beat's* headline, 'Carnegie Hall Gets First Taste of Swing', was quite accurate.

Olin Downes, music critic of *The New York Times*, admitted his anticipatory misgivings in his review the next morning; he had taken his seat with 'a thumping of the heart.' He was more impressed with the excitement and enthusiasm of the audience than he was with the music: 'There is hardly an attempt at beauty of tone,' he wrote, 'and certainly none at construction of melody.' In the end he found it 'decidedly monotonous.' The reviewer of the *Herald Tribune* was more favorable, though describing himself as 'an incompletely initiated listener.'

That night the Goodman band had probably been at top potential and stronger than ever before or afterwards in personnel.

Sadly, there had been turnover and was to be much more. Not many jazz bands could keep the same members together for long. Precisely who, then, comprised the Goodman organization at Carnegie Hall? First, there were the Trio and Quartet consisting of Benny himself, Krupa, Wilson, and Hampton. Benny and Gene also played in the full band. Its other members were:

*Trumpets:* Harry James, Ziggy Elman, and Chris Griffin – perhaps the most effective trumpet trio in swing history.

*Trombones:* Red Ballard and Vernon Brown.

*Alto Saxophones:* Hymie Schertzer and George Koenig.

*Tenor Saxophones:* Art Rollini and Babe Russin.

*Bass:* Harry Goodman.

*Guitar:* Allan Reuss.

*Piano:* Jess Stacy.

*Vocalist:* Martha Tilton.

**IF**or other bands which he formed later in his career, Benny often managed to select musicians of comparable quality. But never again did he succeed in keeping such a redoubtable array for any length of time. One thing which made this increasingly difficult was the economic factor; rival bandleaders stood ready to bid high for the services of one's own star performers. Also, it was inevitable that the best men in a group would be tempted, as time went by, to start bands of their own. But still more damaging to unity was the psychological strain in remaining uninterruptedly with one particular band. Boredom could set in when, for instance, you found yourself playing the same song for the ninety-ninth time. Worse yet, personal frictions occurred; and these were aggravated by enforced proximity.

Jazz musicians can be somewhat touchy and high strung. This has been true of Benny himself. To play music wholeheartedly opens you up in some strange way: it makes you feel wonderful at the time, but rather vulnerable afterwards. Performing night after night with the same group of colleagues is bound to produce tensions, jealousies, misunderstandings. It can hardly be called surprising that a number of musicians have taken to drink or worse. Certain of Benny's friends made sacrifices of themselves in this way: it was as if they had offered up their flesh on altars of alcohol or narcotics.

**P**erhaps the closest of Benny's professional relationships was with Gene Krupa. The work which they so often did together on *Sing, Sing, Sing* powerfully underlined their intermittent and yet musically intense partnership. Benny feels that he has never known a more conscientious musician; and besides musicianship Gene had extraordinary tact. There were many times, when Benny was feeling moody or low, that Gene helped him to get on track again. Gene had looked out for the other men in the band too, acting as peacemaker when they felt they were being driven too hard or troubles of other kinds were brewing.

And yet Benny and Gene broke – perhaps inevitably. It happened in March 1938 after a performance at the Earle Theater in Philadelphia. During that engagement, it had become clearer than ever that the customers who crammed the theater worshipped Gene like a hero. Benny hoped that they might show the good sense, if not the generosity, to honor the band as a working entity rather than for one of its members alone. But there was no way he could control the crowd or break its fixation on Gene, and he therefore studiously ignored what was happening. But the situation became intolerable. At the end of the week's run, Gene quit the band. Benny almost immediately replaced him with an old school pal from Chicago, Davey Tough, who had been playing for Bunny Berigan. Davey was a volatile man, extremely sensitive, torn between music and literature, and given to agonizing bouts of drunkenness. He lacked Gene's jumping showmanship and propulsiveness, yet brought to the band a subtle elasticity of his own. For evidence of Davey's highly personal powers on drums, one has only to hear again the record which he cut with Benny and Teddy Wilson toward the end of that harsh and crucial month of March. The title was *Sweet Lorraine*.

In mid-April, Gene Krupa launched a new band of his own at the Marine Ballroom of Atlantic City's Steel Pier. Spurred on by Gene's own passionate and superb drumming, the band displayed high-pressure drive right from the start, and evoked ecstatic responses from the audience. Benny was glad to hear of this. The public had begun to develop a craving for swing, and at the top of the frenziedly swaying music tree there was room enough for an old and valued friend.

Benny's band also appeared at the Steel Pier, later on in the same year. Davey Tough celebrated the occasion by performing a fine drum solo on an old favorite of the orchestra's: *Don't Be That Way*. The crowd all but booed Davey's effort; they seemed to remember Gene Krupa taking the break more excitingly. Feeling the chill, Davey asked Benny if they couldn't play the tune again. The second time around, he two-stroked it, giving what appeared to be a reasonable facsimile of Krupa's technique. The crowd, thinking it recognized the style, went wild with delight. In fact, Davey's imitation was a put-on. He had managed to translate Krupa's complex rendering into a childishly easy turn; and at least the band enjoyed the joke.

**B**efore the year was out, Benny and Gene publicly buried their differences. It happened again in Philadelphia. Gene's band was playing at the Arcadia Restaurant when Benny brought his in for a brief theater engagement. Gene sent word to the theater, inviting the whole Goodman band to visit the Arcadia as his personal guests. The invitation was too generous to resist and they all went over after the show at the theater. Benny and Gene found themselves reconciled once and for all, right there on the Arcadia's bandstand.

In 1942, when Gene was convicted in California on a charge of contributing to the delinquency of a minor (he was in possession of marijuana), Benny went straight out from New York to visit him in prison. The first thing he said was that if Gene ever cared to rejoin the Goodman band, he would be welcomed with cheers from every man. When Krupa finally won his appeal and was released after almost a year in prison with an ironically clean record, it was financially unfeasible for him to put his own band together again, so he took up Benny's offer. They celebrated their temporary reunion with a tour of military installations, during which Gene characteristically donated his salary to the U.S.O. Toward the end of 1943, Benny settled in with his band at the Ice Terrace Room of the Hotel New Yorker, and Gene was there again at his drums.

As a bandleader, Benny was often accused of downplaying the lyrics of his songs. He seemed to care almost too much for the music itself, relegating 'the vocal' to the status of just another chorus. The talented Helen Forrest, in particular, charged him with that; and she was not with the band long. She left 'in order to avoid a nervous breakdown,' as she put it, and joined Harry James.

But there was no serious shortage of other good girl vocalists. Take, for example, the first Helen: Helen Ward. Back in Chicago in 1936, while at the Urban Room of the Congress Hotel, Helen Ward and the band had cut a stack of records together with the greatest pleasure. There was something wonderfully sprightly and springlike about Helen Ward's rendition of Johnny Mercer's *Goody-Goody*, say, or *It's Been So Long*, or the one that she sang with the Trio called *Too Good To Be True*. Helen Ward, described in a 1936 ad as 'America's Premier Orchestra Bluestress,' left only to get married and settle down; she's been loyal ever since, and even now keeps in touch.

Then, too, there was the girl who replaced Helen Forrest in the summer of 1941; her name was Norma Egstrom but she became Peggy Lee. Later in their relationship, Peggy admitted that there were certain songs which she would have preferred to present in a style different from the one Benny required. But she was not distressed by that: on the contrary, she says her work with him helped her to learn about give-and-take in music. One of the first recordings she made with Benny was Eddie Sauter's subtle and rather difficult arrangement of *I See A Million People*. While singing it, she sounded literally afraid of going wrong somehow, like a small girl alone in a strange mansion of sounds; but this only enhances the poignancy of the song itself. It was also with Benny and the band, in 1942, that she recorded her first authentic hit, *Why Don't You Do Right?*

Peggy Lee was one of the many girls who sang with the band during the long period of its public performing, but Benny recorded with a great many other vocalists of various kinds. One in particular he remembers with affection: Jimmy Rushing, whom he borrowed from Count Basie's band in order to record an Irving Berlin song as soon as it came out in 1936. The lyrics of *He Ain't Got Rhythm* suited Jimmy's booting style.

He had a rich, warm, mocking voice, with an unsettling turbulence just below the surface. He was called 'Mr Five by Five' because he was built precisely along those lines, resembling a brown rubber ball, bouncing with confidence. He generally knew in advance just how he wanted to present a song: there wasn't much for the bandleader to do, just to see to it that an appropriate musical background was sketched in.

Years later, in 1958, Russ Connor, the discographer, suggested to Benny that he take Rushing along on a European tour. Benny was not convinced of the outcome, but Russ turned out to be right. European audiences had never before seen or heard an exuberant performance of the kind that Jimmy Rushing gave every time. At the American Pavilion on the grounds of the Brussels World's Fair, more than once he came close to stealing the show. He was an irresistibly appealing performer, and Benny was proud to have him on his team.

And yet Benny cannot help thinking of Rushing as a brass-lunged Johnny-one-note. His reaction to Bessie Smith is not noticeably different. Benny's personal preference has always been for singers of a more versatile and less booming kind. Oddly enough, he actually worked with Bessie Smith, on her last recording date, in November 1933. Public interest in Bessie then, and up until her violent death a few years afterwards, had virtually vanished. Hot musicians still admired her, and the men who assembled in the studio to back her up on that particular afternoon were all outstanding. The date had been organized by Buck Washington, of the old 'Buck and Bubbles' team. The group was made up of Chu Berry on tenor sax, Frankie Newton on trumpet, Jack Teagarden on trombone, Benny, and Buck himself on piano. Bessie belted out four songs which suited her imperious voice. *Gimme A Pigfoot* came first, followed by the humorous and mildly salacious *Do Your Duty*. Then it was *Take Me For A Buggy Ride*, and a truly traditional blues, *I'm Down In The Dumps*, the opening lines of which went like this:

*I heard a knock on my do'*
*Las' night when I was 'sleep*

*I thought it was that sweet man of mine,*
*Makin' his fo-day creep.*
*Wasn't nothing but the landlord,*
*That great big chump!*
*Stay 'way from my do', Mr. Landlord,*
*'Cause I'm down in the dumps!*

In spite of Bessie's great fame afterwards, Benny finds that his predilection is for subtler musicianship than Bessie was able to give. Ella Fitzgerald, for example, has always been one of his favorites.

Ella seems to him the sweetest female voice in jazz music, one who relates to people in some positive way not only as a singer but also as a human being. Away back in 1936 he borrowed her from Chick Webb's orchestra in order to record *Did You Mean It?* During the same session they made *Take Another Guess* and something especially beautiful: *Goodnight My Love.* Into those songs Ella put absolute sincerity, something you could not fake in a million years.

It had turned out that Ella was at the time under contract to a different recording company, a fact which caused embarrassing difficulties. The records had to be withdrawn from sale and for decades remained unavailable. While Benny may look on that sort of incident as one of the inevitable problems of life, a truly sympathetic and creative session with Ella and the band was something you could not buy for money.

Billie Holiday was out of another mold. She possessed a tongue with a tang, and even to corny songs she imparted a kind of mordancy. Billie was Ella's peer, yet she seemed a more ambiguous character. Benny first became aware of her through John Hammond at a tiny gin-mill on 137th Street in Harlem, when she was only seventeen, fresh from Baltimore, fresh and ebullient by nature. At the time when they shared a couple of recording sessions in 1935, they occasionally went out together to some of the Harlem spots; but they soon drifted apart again.

Many years later, when he happened to catch her performances, Benny had the impression that Billie's talent and ability were growing more individual, more expressive, year by year. Her singing became increasingly lonely, ravaged, virginal – all three at once. She sounded far away; remote and yet shatteringly personal – like a nightingale singing in the dark depths of a forest. Toward the end of her life she became a truly tragic figure, a travesty of all her young aspirations. From Benny's point of view, however, Billie's masochistic love life and her suicidal use of drugs were not the important things. What mattered finally was her capacity for expressing the human tragedy in song.

**E**lla and Billie were two of the true queens among vocalists in the heyday of jazz. A third was Mildred Bailey, best known for her work with her husband, Red Norvo. Benny regularly featured her on his 'Camel Caravan' broadcasts from New York in 1939. Mildred Bailey was huge on her tiny feet, like a captive balloon hissing with 250 lbs. of helium, and volatile. Her arms, her intellect, her voice, all seemed to embrace the music. Mildred was able to work with a big band while keeping her individuality intact. That might seem to be a fairly commonplace achievement, but in fact only a few singers could do it. Powerful vocal cords were not required: the mikes and amplifiers took care of that. What was needed above all was a good strong temperament in order to capture a song and make it your own.

Another old friend and colleague (now departed) whom Benny looks back on with great affection is Johnny Mercer, singer and perhaps one of the most remarkable lyricists to have emerged in America. In the period when Johnny appeared with some regularity on radio programs he would improvise lyrics to a blues rhythm on events of the preceding week, such as the Indianapolis races, or whatever, and he was never caught short of an apt and ingenious rhyme. For Benny he had been a delight to work with, delivering his own best material with a gusto such as only a slightly mad creative talent could summon. *Cuckoo In The Clock*, for example: they had recorded that together in February 1939, and Benny managed to imitate the cuckoo notes of the lyrics on clarinet. It was on that same afternoon that they also waxed a deservedly famous number, *And The Angels Sing*, based on a gusty Jewish song. Johnny Mercer and Ziggy Elman devised it together, and Martha Tilton was the vocalist. She gave the song her characteristic lilting performance backed up all the way by Ziggy's own ecstatic trumpet breaks. The result was a triumph, small in scope yet genuine; words and music had been brought to dovetail perfectly. So had the male and female leading roles – Ziggy's and Martha's – in performance. It was one of the real highlights of that period in Benny's career.

It was in Las Vegas in March 1942 that Benny was married to Alice Hammond, whom he had first met in 1938 in Boston. Benny was 33, a bachelor, wedded to music, as someone put it. Alice was from a patrician family, the sister of John Hammond, and she was the divorced wife of a prominent Englishman. Some of their friends found it difficult to believe the news. The consensus seems to have been that Alice showed courage in marrying him, and Benny agrees. If a musician were to hit too many sour notes, you would let him go; you could not fire a marriage partner.

When they drove off on their honeymoon that night in Las Vegas, Benny was exhausted and after a while he turned the wheel over to Alice. He climbed across to the back seat, curled up and fell asleep. At the California border, around midnight, state policemen stopped the car and asked Alice what she was carrying. Benny, half awake, heard her calm reply: 'My husband.'

Alice calculated later that, during the first four months of their marriage, they slept under no fewer than 73 different roofs. It was remarkable that she had managed to put up with it, for Alice was a nester, the sort of person whose first instinct is to settle in somewhere and immediately create a warm beautiful surrounding. She approached the challenges and promises of home life as an artist, even in the years during the War when they were living in Los Angeles and Benny was making films.

Eventually they actually had three homes. In New York, Benny was in charge and shouldered full responsibility. In Connecticut and the Dutch Antilles, however, they arranged things differently. There, Alice set the pace, and there Benny relaxed. She helped him to forget worldly cares, and yet, paradoxically, she also helped him to see them more clearly. They had two daughters, Rachel and Benjie, the one interested in music, the second an artist. Benny tried to put something of his feelings for the girls into music; he wrote and performed tributes of love to them in his own fashion. One was called *Rachel's Dream*, another *Benjie's Bubble*. And for Alice's three daughters by her first marriage he wrote *Hi 'Ya Sophia*, *Shirley Steps Out* and *Gilly*.

**B**enny has always thought that temperament is a most peculiar thing. No artist can get very far without it, and yet temperaments vary enormously from star to star. In the 1940s he appeared in a Billy rose production called *The Seven Lively Arts*. Among others the cast included Beatrice Lillie, Bert Lahr and the extraordinary Doc

Rockwell, each of whom took a different attitude towards the show. For Beatrice Lillie, to begin with, it was intensely involving as well as fun. She was always alert to audience reactions, and modified each performance according to the response she felt. A theater star through and through, she drew her best strength from laughter.

By contrast Bert Lahr was a Pagliacci, a tormented clown. Each night he would walk out on stage like a man going to his doom in a bad dream – and then he would invariably win the audience with his overwhelming talent. On the other hand the insouciant Doc Rockwell was always in easy control of the situation and never given to nerves.

In the preparation of the show it was decided that Benny and the other three stars would take their bows together at the end in eighteenth-century pastel-colored costumes. Benny firmly declined to wear the prescribed outfit, arguing that his contribution to the show was supposed to be musical and not comic. Billy Rose, over-optimistic and used to having his own way, presumed that in the end Benny would climb down and follow the plan.

Sitting with Alice in the audience, on opening night at the Ziegfeld Theater, Billy Rose was all smiles until the curtain calls. When Benny came on for his bow in the same dinner-jacket he had worn throughout the show, Rose climbed halfway out of his aisle seat muttering, 'That no-good son of a bitch!' Benny received a stiff note from Rose, stating that henceforth no one would be permitted to take a curtain call except in full costume. That happened to suit Benny; now he had a written and signed excuse to go home early every night, skipping the final curtain altogether. Billy Rose was naturally furious, but realized on reflection that he had been out-flanked and there was nothing further he could do.

The story points up a paradoxical aspect of Benny's own temperament. On the one hand, he has been known as a worrier and a workhorse who puts out more of himself the tougher things get. Even in the great days of the 1930s, according to no less an authority than Harry James, Benny was accustomed to practise his instrument 'fifteen times more than the entire Goodman orchestra combined.' But Benny has also displayed an opposite tendency, often withdrawing. Why that should be he has never been able to say. The habit of withdrawal has interfered with some of his favorite projects, and even chilled a few cherished relationships over the years.

For instance there was a sad contretemps with Louis Armstrong. Benny sometimes regretted the fact that he and Louis so seldom collaborated in performance. The first time they got together professionally was in 1939. Louis sang *Ain't Misbehavin'*, as only he could do it, on Benny's 'Camel Caravan' radio program. Six years later, Louis, Duke Ellington and Benny all joined forces on a radio round-up show. Broadcasting simultaneously from New York, New Orleans and San Francisco, they performed the Duke's *Things Ain't What They Used To Be* while listening to each other on earphones. At one point Benny heard a phrase of his bounce back across the continent, thought it came from Louis, and echoed it again on clarinet. Across thousands of miles on radio there had been a crazy, confusing closeness.

Then in 1947 Louis and Benny did sporadic work together on a Hollywood film of no great consequence called *A Song Is Born*, starring Danny Kaye. Benny appeared as 'Professor Magenbruch' – a square in a curly little mustache. Virginia Mayo was supposed in the story to convert the Professor to hot music. Benny was hardly unaware of Hollywood's crass commercial nature. He understood that to work there meant participating in daydreams for money; all the same, certain episodes seemed rather embarrassing to him. Louis, however, appeared to enjoy all of it.

Perhaps indeed he had. Benny wonders if that might have been the secret of Armstrong's sorcery. Could it have been nothing but joy, simple, unconfined joy, which enabled Louis to rise above his surroundings and make them appear magically more than they actually were?

In 1953, Benny invited Louis to participate in a tour of the United States. The time seemed ripe because Benny's and Louis' old records were being released again as LP albums and selling remarkably well. For the tour Benny collected a band which consisted almost entirely of old friends and familiar faces. Gene Krupa was on drums, as in the old days. Helen Ward was again vocalist. Ziggy Elman, Charlie Shavers and Al Stewart comprised the trumpet section. Georgie Auld, Sol Schlinger, Clint Neagley and Willie Smith were the sax men. On trombone there were Vernon Brown and Rex Peer. Best of all, it seemed to Benny at the time, Louis agreed to come along bringing reinforcements in the shape of a small group of his own. There was every reason to think that their tour would be able to offer the very finest traditional jazz – black and white together – in one irresistible package.

The tour opened in Boston and then went on to New York for its first real test in Carnegie Hall. The audience was middle-aged, and seemed to have come in a remembering mood, not to enjoy the music so much as to compare it with former performances and to sit in judgment. Louis went out first to face them. He walked on stage with his characteristic gait, as if treading clouds of variable density, lifting each foot high off the floor and grinning rather fiercely. Then setting his trumpet aside he proceeded to tell a story which, to put it as finely as possible, was off-color. The vulgar punch-line brought only a little laughter followed by a patter of applause. Many people seemed not to have understood the joke, let alone the spirit behind it.

The idea of the tour had been dreamed up by eager managers, who saw an obvious opportunity for profit. But Benny had been out of the musical scene for a while; it was difficult for him to contemplate a long series of two shows a night, lasting from 7 p.m. to 1 a.m., in an assortment of cities. Louis was less bothered by this, being a 'showman personified,' as Benny has expressed it. Benny felt it was better to bow out at the start of the tour, rather than endure pressures which were no longer necessary to him.

Benny has been perfectly able to endure other pressures and disputes when he has been on the receiving end. Fellow performers have walked out on him, and he knows from experience how this can hurt. In 1941, for example, he was scheduled to appear with the Philadelphia Symphony Orchestra at its summer open-air auditorium, Robin Hood Dell. José Iturbi, best known as a rather flashy pianist, was to conduct the program, but angrily opted out when he learned that Benny was to be the soloist on the basis that Benny was no more than a jazz man. In the event, Kirsten Flagstad's accompanist, Edwin McArthur, was substituted as conductor, 14,000 people packed the stadium, and the concert was accounted a resounding success.

On one occasion long ago, Benny finished a dance hall gig in Wisconsin and immediately boarded a bus to Chicago in order to keep a recording date with the Pro Arte ensemble. This was probably the finest string quartet in the world at that time, and Benny had never played with them before. When he arrived at the studio, where they were scheduled to perform Mozart's *Quintet*, he suddenly realized what it would mean to record this work without any proper rehearsals, and he said to himself, 'This isn't right.' Politely he bowed and left the studio; and left the city as well.

**B**ut these embarrassing experiences have been relatively few in Benny's professional life. He prefers to concentrate on happier times, such as the historic tour of Russia, in 1962, even though this too had its distressing aspects. The tour was promoted and guaranteed by cultural exchange officials in Washington, who had asked Benny to handle the whole thing. But he soon found himself under political pressures and interference. Having never thought of race at all in his life, Benny was asked to 'make sure' that the band he took with him included a good number of black musicians. In fact some of those he enlisted were most reluctant to go.

He was next informed that he was to negotiate the players' salaries, and that he himself would perform without compensation. Benny had given his free services to hundreds of benefits in the past, but this tour had not been conceived as a venture in international charity. The Moscow bureaucrats also turned out to be remarkably insensitive. One of the first things they did was to inform Benny that the band would be required to play each night of the trip. Benny, however, personally camped on the doorstep of the Commissar of Culture until he obtained some slight mitigation of this extraordinary condition.

Within the band there also proved to be certain difficulties. Some of the musicians seemed inclined to offer styles of performance which Benny could not tolerate, and it took all his firmness as leader to get his point of view across. Finally, as most people know from press coverage of the event, the dictator of the time, Nikita

Khrushchev, made some humorously philistine remarks to Benny regarding jazz in general. A statesman might have understood how to argue Khrushchev to a standstill on the relative merits of American and Russian refrigerators or automobiles, but Benny did not care to debate matters of music. The work they did on that tour all over Russia should speak for itself, he felt, and so it had done to the people themselves. That was what made the trip so memorable. There was no question at all about the reaction of Russian audiences; they opened up to the music like flowers in spring and Benny felt happy among them. Perhaps it was his Russian heritage that had something to do with that.

By the time of that tour of Russia, Benny had already undertaken several foreign visits as a kind of goodwill semi-official cultural representative of the United States. He had a huge success with the band at the Brussels International Exposition of 1958. Then in 1964 he went to Japan with pianist Dick Shreve, bass player Monty Budwig and drummer Colin Bailey. These men were not well known at the time but played fine music, something the Japanese recognized at once, and they welcomed the group with open arms. Even during a bitterly cold night in February when the group were playing at the Kosei Nenkin auditorium in Tokyo and something had gone wrong with the heating system, the audience, wearing hats and coats, coughing and sneezing, nevertheless reacted excitedly to the group, and particularly to *Stompin' At The Savoy*, which brought shout upon shout of 'Banzai!'

**T**his kind of success, even in unpromising circumstances, is fairly typical of Benny's life and career. He has been fortunate too in the people he has known, both professionally and personally. In the classical field he has learnt a great deal from certain instrumentalists, particularly Joseph Szigeti, Reginald Kell, Gus Langenus and members of the Budapest String Quartet. On the jazz scene dozens of his friends and early colleagues have succeeded far beyond his, and their, wildest dreams. Trumpeter Harry James, who gave so much to the Goodman band in the late 1930s, subsequently became a rival bandleader of the most formidable kind. Harry has remained a leader ever since, and his career has been thoroughly distinguished. He has been known to complain that he never understood Benny; perhaps this was mutual. Musically, however, they were always comrades.

As for the original Goodman Quartet, each of Benny's associates in that group went on to lead a band in his own right. Each, moreover, found fame and fortune in doing so. Mel Powell, who was Benny's favorite pianist in the 1940s and early 1950s, achieved distinction in another way, by becoming Dean of the California Institute of Arts.

To be, as Benny was, the sort of leader who helps to shape new leaders is gratifying on the whole, despite the personal wrenches that were sometimes involved. Stan Kenton, an adventurous and generally progressive bandleader, once described the situation pungently in an interview: 'You bring a young musician along,' he said, 'you nurse him – and all of a sudden he tells you to get lost and flies away. It's beautiful!'

Like Harry James, Stan Kenton seems in no mood for retirement yet. Nor are Count Basie, Woody Herman, or Buddy Rich. Why should they be? Young people seem to be flocking to hear what bandleaders of the old school have to offer. Amazingly enough, three decades after Glenn Miller's disappearance in World War II, the Glenn Miller orchestra still draws large audiences. There have always been, and always will be, popular trends in music. That does little to change the fact that the very best music of each generation is likely to hold its own up and down the line.

In some ways Benny feels that classical performances are still the most rewarding. There was even a time when he would have accepted steady work in that line, for instance with the Boston Symphony Orchestra under Serge Koussevitsky; but leading a jazz group at places like the Rainbow Room in New York could also be pleasant. You knew your colleagues, and the crowd, and they knew you as well. That gave a comfortable feeling to the whole enterprise: people seemed happy and you had a sense that you were helping them to be that way. Concert tours were obviously tougher. The challenge of assembling a jazz combo and getting it to swing abroad was almost irresistible, yet sometimes Benny wished he had resisted after all. A tour he made not long ago in Australia, for example, was a delight – but what an endless distance he had to cover!

Of the places where Benny has performed outside of the United States, on balance he likes London's Albert Hall best of all. His most recent appearance there was hailed with true and unflappable British reserve, in the *Sunday Times*, as 'outrageously good.'

The group he brought to London deserved a large part of the credit. Tenor sax man Zoot Sims had started with him at the tender age of seventeen, in 1943. Zoot seems to have done nothing but improve since then; he plays his deliberately unpolished instrument in marvellously supple yet solid style. Bucky Pizarelli is a prince among guitarists; infinitely more playful than most, he keeps himself curiously in check at the same time. Peter Appleyard, too, promises and delivers silver plenties of music. His vibe hammering is crisp, enthusiastic, showmanly. He happens besides to be a Londoner himself, born and bred not far from Albert Hall. Appleyard's family had never heard him perform before that night and they were in the front row.

Granting the obvious fact that any man is bound to lose some bounce over the years, Benny tells himself that he has gained a lot at the same time. Self knowledge keeps deepening; so does his understanding of the instrument. Finally, one learns self denial. That increased discipline makes one's improvisations suppler and more delicate. One's tone is truer as well. Not one listener in a hundred would even notice that, but what difference? The pleasure of the audience is not the main thing. No, to be quite honest about it, the thing that matters most is simply one's own satisfaction and joy in blowing beautiful sounds. The musicians Benny most admires all have felt the same way he does about that. The jazz artists among them jammed for fun and for free, when the occasion arose. The classical instrumentalists would get together for chamber music sessions in exactly the same spirit. They loved music, not so much the public. Nor did they tend to torment themselves about posterity's verdict on their work. Music at its best was a happening, not a monument.

Benny has always tried to keep that point in mind at recording sessions. To try and perform something definitively is a mistake. Things done 'for the ages' sound ageless – never young or fresh. It is better to treat each recording as a first time round. In 1963, for example, Benny brought his original Goodman Quartet together in that spirit. They looked at each other, perhaps thinking that no one of the four was youthful any longer; and then settled in to play as if each had been born yesterday. The tunes they chose were 'oldies' in the main, jazz numbers which have become classics of a kind in the course of a generation or so. But once again the men treated them as new; and the result was good music.

Benny's most recent exercise in 'going back' was the commemorative Carnegie Hall concert he put together, with the help of his friends, on 17 January 1978. If anybody needed reassurance that Benny's name had retained its golden glow and that the swing band era was far from forgotten, this concert provided the affirmative answer: the whole house was sold out on the day tickets went on sale. And the event itself proved a climax of his late career.

The publicity leading up to the concert was enormous: articles in leading newspapers and magazines; a *New Yorker* special by Whitney Balliett; announcements in all the media. For the concert itself, there was an attempt to reassemble as many of the original musicians as possible; Benny hoped at first that Jess Stacy (now retired), Teddy Wilson, Vernon Brown and Harry James might be on hand; in the event only Lionel Hampton and Martha Tilton were able to join Benny as representatives of the 1938 group.

In mapping out the concert, Benny made no attempt to repeat the program of forty years before. The only nostalgic numbers were the signature tune, *Let's Dance*, Martha Tilton's repeat of her greatest single success, *Loch Lomond*, and the rousing tribute to the late Gene Krupa, *Sing, Sing, Sing*. As an event, it certainly worked; as a musical evening, it was not all that might have been hoped for. But the tribute written by the critic John S. Wilson in the *New York Times* on 19 January made a gratifying point about Benny Goodman as a musician today. After discussing the shortcomings of the performance and calling the group 'lack luster' and missing 'the fire and spirit of the real Goodman band,' Wilson went on to praise Benny's performance of contemporary songs such as *Yesterday* and *Send In The Clowns*:

Despite work in an aura of nostalgia for the last thirty years, the past seems to have slipped away from Benny Goodman. He functions most effectively now in the present, which, for a creative artist, is always the best place to be.

Alice died after a short illness in February 1978; and her absence naturally makes a difference. But in 1979 Benny is a young 70-year-old. He has a heavy schedule of engagements, for performances of 'serious' music as well as jazz with a group of artists who usually include Warren Vache on trumpet, Buddy Tate on tenor sax, John Bunch on piano, Cal Collins on guitar, Connie Kaye on drums, Major Holley on bass, and Scott Hamilton on sax. His name and his music turn up all the time. In 1978, for example, Bob Fosse put on a big Broadway show called *Dancin'*, the hit of which many people consider to be a sequence called 'Benny's Number,' based on the 1938 Carnegie Hall recording of *Sing, Sing, Sing*. The *New Yorker* dance critic, Arlene Croce, wrote of it, 'The music is a powerhouse that shakes Fosse loose from some of his mannerisms,' and called it 'the big killer in the show.'

And ahead? There seems to be no reason why Benny should not go on as long as he likes doing what he started doing in the early days in Chicago, that incredible seedbed of great jazz musicians. Indeed, it is what his whole life has consisted of – just making music.

# GROWING UP

Benny Goodman at the age of 10. Long
on talent if still in short pants, he was gaining attention
in Chicago's theaters with his imitation of that popular
and extrovert entertainer Ted Lewis ('Is everybody happy?')
*Next page :* The Hull House Boys' Club band, around 1920.
Benny is in the photograph though difficult to identify
confidently. Benny believes he is the boy
just left of center whose head is framed in a doorway.

Studio portraits of Benny and his brother Harry, presumably taken
in about 1926. Harry first played tuba and then what
Benny calls 'the bass fiddle.' He was a member of Ben Pollack's
band along with Benny in the early days, and later was bassist in
Benny's own band. Harry now resides in Southern France.

**Benny Goodman with five of his brothers :**
Louis, Irving, Eugene, Freddie and the youngest, Jerome, Benny's favorite.
*Opposite :* **Dora and David Goodman, Benny's parents. The father is shown here
as a young man, photographed shortly after his arrival in Baltimore from Russia.
Mrs. Goodman, who survived her husband by a great many years, is shown in a
photograph taken in Chicago in the 1930s. Though not a musician, David
Goodman loved music, and bought a Victrola for the family even when he had
difficulty earning enough money for their food. This immigrant couple produced
12 children, four of whom proved to have musical talents (Freddie and Irving
both played trumpet, in addition to Harry on the bass and Benny on the clarinet).
Benny's overwhelming success and fame went far beyond anything that either of
his parents could have hoped for.**

**Benny and his mother in the 1940s. A decade
earlier Benny established her in New York, where her
bountiful kitchen often fed Benny's struggling bandsmen.**
*Opposite :* **A proud Mrs. Goodman with five of her sons, Benny in the
middle.
Benny and Jerome in the early 1930s. Jerome was killed in a plane
crash in 1944 while serving in the U.S. Army Air Corps.**

Three members of Ben Pollack's band in a display of high spirits,
each pretending to play an instrument other than the one he was accustomed to : Benny
Goodman, Fud Livingston and Gil Rodin. Though Benny was never much of a performer
on the flute, he did in fact play saxophone and a bit of trumpet in the early days.
*Opposite :* Benny in a studio portrait taken in New York when he was about 20.
By this time he was wearing eyeglasses.

*Above :* **The Pollack band in early 1927, probably in the Southmoor Hotel, Chicago. Benny is seated next to drummer Pollack, and Glenn Miller is sitting farthest right in back row.**
*Opposite :* **Another portrait of Benny in New York just after the Pollack band came east for the first time.**

*Opposite above :* **The Ben Pollack band in October 1928, when they were appearing at the Park Central Hotel in New York. From left to right are Al Harris, Ed Bergman, Harry Goodman, Larry Binyon, Jim McPartland, Benny Goodman, Dick Morgan, Jack Teagarden, Vic Briedis, Vic Moore, Gil Rodin. Ben Pollack is seated.**
*Opposite below :* **One of the earliest photographs of 'Ben Pollack and his Californians'. Farthest left is Glenn Miller, and next to him is Benny Goodman. Harry Goodman is third from the right. The time is early 1927.**
*Above :* **A photograph typical of Atlantic City, half a century before the intrusion of gambling casinos. The Ben Pollack band in rolling chairs on the boardwalk in front of Million Dollar Pier (1927).**

*Opposite* : **Benny Goodman in August 1930 at Gages Lake, Illinois.**
*Below* : **An early example of the kind of publicity Benny was to receive throughout his lifetime.**
*Bottom* : **A rare Goodman collector's item : cover of a publication of jazz breaks transcribed by Benny, which first appeared in 1927 when he was only 18 years old. (Photo courtesy Phil Kidby)**

Before Swing—Benny, Dick Morgan and brother Henry.

From the album—Benny with Jimmy Dorsey (left).

Taken in 1930—Benny, brother Charlie and his family.

BENNY
GOODMAN'S
125 JAZZ BREAKS
FOR THE
SAXOPHONE and CLARINET

HERMAN DAREWSKI MUSIC PUBLISHING CO.,
9-10, New Compton Street, London, W.C.2.
AMERICA: MELROSE MUSIC CORP., NEW YORK.
Authorised for sale and distribution in England, Ireland, Scotland, Wales, India and British Possessions in Africa.
MADE IN ENGLAND

PRICE
4/-

A recording session in 1934, in which the group consisted of Dick McDonough, Sonny Lee, Charlie Margulis, Mannie Klein, Coleman Hawkins, Benny, Artie Bernstein, and producer Milt Gabler. Benny was among the first white jazz leaders to use black musicians in his recording sessions.

# THE SWINGING YEARS

The Paramount Theatre (now demolished) will
always be one of the primary symbols of the swinging years.
It was here that many of the big name bands
appeared – in those palmy days when cinemagoers were
offered not just a first-run film but 'live'
entertainment as well – and more specifically it was here
that the Benny Goodman band established
itself in 1937 as the most popular of them all.
For several years Benny and the band appeared
at the Paramount repeatedly ; the marquee in this photograph
announces one of their engagements in early 1939.

In December 1935 the band began a successful engagement at the Congress Hotel in Chicago. Originally booked for two weeks, the band was kept on for six months. The vocalist shown here was Helen Ward. The two dancing couples at right were photographed in the studio of the 'Let's Dance' radio program which featured three bands on a five-hour nationwide network. On the left Benny Goodman is dancing with Helen Ward, on the right one of the announcers with singer Connie Bates. The period is around December 1934. (NBC photo, courtesy Frank Driggs, Helen Ward Collection)

In August 1935 the Benny Goodman band undertook a
transcontinental tour, and are shown here during an engagement in Denver,
Colorado. The tour was depressing and largely unsuccessful until the
band hit Los Angeles where their performances at the Palomar Ballroom made
their reputation. Bunny Berigan is seated directly below Benny.
*Right :* **After the Chicago engagement in 1936 the band
was in Hollywood appearing in a film called** *The Big Broadcast Of 1937*
*Overleaf :* **The engagement shown here was at the Stanley Theatre in
Pittsburgh, and took place in 1935. Note, under the main marquee, the
reference to the group as a 'radio orchestra,' acknowledgment of the band's
popular 'Let's Dance' program.**

*Left :* **Fletcher Henderson (known affectionately as 'Smack'), whose arrangements played a large part in setting the tone of the Benny Goodman orchestra.**
*Below :* **A photograph of** *The Big Broadcast Of 1937* **band, consisting of Hymie Schertzer, Red Ballard, Pee Wee Erwin, Gene Krupa, Harry Goodman, Jess Stacy, Murray McEachern, Benny Goodman, Art Rollini, Nate Kazebier, Bill DePew, Chris Griffin, Allan Reuss and Dick Clark.**

Left : **A composite publicity photograph prepared for the Paramount
picture** The Big Broadcast Of 1937 **featuring Benny and Leopold Stokowski.
A 1936 ad for the Robbins Music Co. sheet music of that great success
of the day,** Stompin' At The 'Savoy.

*Opposite above :* **A supper-club party in about 1937 including that gifted trumpeter, Bunny Berigan** *(left)*, **who was a member of the Goodman band for a short time, successfully established his own band, and died at an extremely young age. Third from the left is the singer Lee Wiley.**
*Opposite below :* **A Goodman family gathering in 1936 at the Hotel Pennsylvania, where Benny and his band were appearing nightly. Benny is sitting between his mother and sister Ethel. At the left are Helen Oakley, the Chicago socialite and promoter of jazz concerts, and the music publisher Jack Bregman.**
*Below :* **A rehearsal for a 'Camel Caravan' broadcast in 1937. The personnel are (at the back) Harry James, Ziggy Elman and Chris Griffin ; and sitting Red Ballard, George Koenig and Hymie Schertzer. Critics acclaim the three-and-a-half-year 'Camel Caravan' series as the best swing music programs ever broadcast.**
*Overleaf :* **The Steel Pier in Atlantic City, mecca for bands like Benny Goodman's. The large photograph, showing Benny's name on the marquee, was taken in 1936. (Alex Bartha's was the 'house band' ; Ziggy Elman left it to join Benny during this engagement.) The inset shows the band inside the Steel Pier, and gives some idea of the enthusiastic crowds that the band was attracting in those days.**

# STEEL PIER

BENNY **GOODMAN** AND H
BAN
JANE WITHERS PEPPER
IRVIN S COBB IN

STEEL PIER

HAT YOU GET FOR ONE MALL DMISSION

DANCING

ALL FOR ONE ADMISSION

LEO CARRILLO
BIG CIRCUS V
MINSTRELS
5 THEA

F E A T U R E | ALICE
PHOTOPLAYS| SENSA
TODAY BENNY GOODMA

5 BIG THEATRES VAUDEVILLE
3 FEATURE PICTURES
Dance 2 CHILDRENS SHOW

LEO CARRILLO
OTHER · VAUDEVILLE · ACTS
BAKER
HIGH DIVING HORSES
BIG
10 DAREDEVIL ACTS
WATER

VAUDEVILLE
MINSTRELS
BIG CIRCUS
DANCING

CHILD

DAVY JONES' See The Parade Of The THE HAUNTED World's Largest MINIATURE MI

BENNY GOODMAN AND HIS ORCHESTRA
STEEL PIER · 1936

IN PERSON
UDEVILLE
DANCING
RES

DIVING
HORSES

AYE ADOLPHE MENJOU IN "SING BABY SING"
IONAL CIRCUS AND WATER SPORTS
AND HIS ORCHESTRA and ALEX BARTHA AND HIS Orchestra

The Steel Pier's Famous
INSTRELS
NOTED STAGE STARS

Steel Pier ZOO
WILD ANIMAL
And Wild Animal Menagerie Of 50.

ENS THEATRE FEATURING JUVENILE REVUE

SOUTH SEAS
MONSTERS

NEW
HOLLYWOOD
EXHIBITS

HEADDRESSES
From All Over

SEE
KONGO
LAND

*Below :* **The line outside the Paramount Theatre waiting to enter to hear the Benny Goodman outfit in January 1939. Note the crown at Benny's left and the message that for the second year the Benny Goodman band had won the 'Paramount Theatre Annual Band Popularity Poll.'**
*Right above :* **A review by George Frazier in** *Down Beat* **of a concert the Goodman band gave in Symphony Hall, Boston, in 1938. Frazier's criticism of the audience for letting their enthusiasm lead them to make too much noise indicates the extent of hysterical popularity which the band had attained. Benny frequently admonished unruly crowds : 'When you quiet down, we'll start to play.'**
*Right below :* **Another indication of the immense popularity of the Benny Goodman band in the 1930s. Here in front of a Detroit movie house, people were obviously waiting overnight to be the first to get into the theater.**

DOWN BEAT

4

# Stupid Critics Misjudge 3,000 Ickies' Action

## Condemn Goodman Because Crowd Goes For Exhibitionism

By George Frazier

Boston, Mass.—If these notes on Benny Goodman's Symphony Hall concert seem sketchy and even inconsistent, it is because the concert itself was just that way. Neither Benny nor the guys, though, should be held accountable for something that was beyond their control.

That something—and, believe me, it was the saddest feature of the proceedings—was the audience reaction. It was flattering, of course, and, in several instances, nothing short of idolatrous. The 3,000 damned distracting too. The 3,000 odd who jammed every available inch of Symphony Hall behaved so bastardly that some magnificent jazz was completely drowned out. The wrong things—that is, the items that inclined toward the killer-diller and the exhibitionistic—were the popular successes of the evening, while the genuine thrills were accorded hardly more than a smattering of polite applause. Musically, the affair failed to maintain the standard set at Carnegie in January, but that, as I say, was largely attributable to the differences between the two audiences.

Where the people at Carnegie were enthusiastic, those at Symphony were downright icky; and I

impeccable taste, he won the gratitude of every true lover of jazz. His tempi were perfect, his composure admirable. He is, of course, so fine that his tremendous worth is not likely to be appreciated by a public weaned on sensationalism; but you had only to listed to the Quartet to realize how stimulating the guy is. I mean this as no slam at Lionel, who played admirably in the Trio. As a matter of fact, the audience seemed to me to be more concerned with Lionel's ability to toss the sticks around than with his musical significance. That, of course, is but another indication of what I have been saying throughout this dispatch.

### Why Doesn't Benny

I don't mean to this business of the tion. After all, w cept the troublin preciative public and that mass ly prove that ciated for its I still regard as worse th me that to necess

### Tough Is Hero; Stacey's Superb

"Dave Tough was in many ways the hero of the evening. Playing with an unbelievable rock and with impeccable taste, he wor the gratitude of every

### Should He Give Up Symphony Hall Concerts?

Benny Goodman

modity. You mention Mildred Bailey and you've disposed of the entire lot of whites. She is, I am sure, the musical personality who is above without a challenger in her Mildred is unavail ing a priceless swell band. Benny's

Brunies is a swell background trombonist—one of the finest in the business, but one suspects his musical integrity when he turns Jim Crow on a superlative drummer like Zutty, whose presence would have made Hackett's band a notable kick.

### No Room in Art for Prejudice

The whole thing gripes me like hell in more ways than one. In the first place, there is no room in art for prejudice. Talent alone should be the requirement and not the color of one's skin. But what is so tragic that it seems incredible is that Zutty, a topnotcher if there ever was one, is without a job. I've heard him sit in at Nick's and I can testify that the crowd approved of him in no uncertain fashion. It was a bitter pill to realize that the only opposition to him existed on the same bandstand.

Both Red Norvo and Benny Goodman left New York for the road April 30 and the town found itself without a really first-class large white band. I found it disturbing that Norvo didn't receive the critical acclaim his swell brand of music warranted. The band (with George Wettling playing marvelous drums) is as relaxed as hell and absolutely tasteful. I've mentioned Mildred above, so there is no need to praise her any further, but a word should be put in about the Norvo reeds. They blend perfectly, swing easy, and can boast of irreproachable intonation. They have a good clarinetist and a swell tenor. The addition of a second trombone has helped the brass immensely and the chief the moment would seem the of a

'Goodmania' in the '30s. This was the style of dancing when the Benny Goodman band was appearing at the Madhattan Room of the Hotel Pennsylvania. Much of the time the enthusiastic audience did not dance, but thronged around the bandsmen to applaud their favorite soloists, whom they knew by name. Others queued patiently for autographs (*Opposite*).
*Bottom :* Two of the talented soloists with the Benny Goodman band at the Hotel Pennsylvania in 1937 : Gene Krupa and Harry James.

*Harry James.*

# HUROK ATTRACTIONS, INC.

## S. HUROK, President
## 30 ROCKEFELLER PLAZA

NEW YORK

January 10th, 1938

Mr. Willard Alexander
Music Corporation of America
745 Fifth Avenue
New York City

Dear Mr. Alexander:

Before leaving for Hollywood this afternoon, I wish to go on record as disapproving of some of the preparations which are being made for Mr. Goodman's Carnegie Hall concert.

I do not think that the idea of Miss Beatrice Lillie acting as commentator is a very good one and believe that it will bring about a certain amount of ridicule from the music critics - who are the very ones you should be seeking to impress.

Also, I am told, you are planning to have Mr. Goodman play against a background of black curtains, with special lighting effects, and with the musicians clad in theatrical costumes. This is contrary to musical tradition and will only serve to neutralize the very dignity which you were seeking to obtain by having Mr. Goodman play at Carnegie Hall.

Since the arrangements with Miss Lillie have already been made, there is no use carping about that point, but I wish to object (since the concert is under my auspices) to the employment of theatrical atmosphere - when the point of this entire event is that it is a concert we are offering, subject to the tradition and decorum of such an event.

Very truly yours,

S. HUROK

copy to: Mr. Benny Goodman

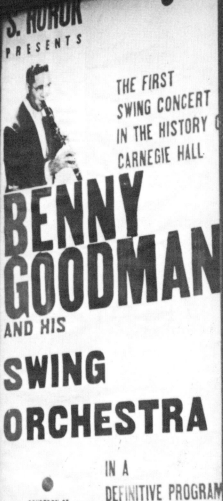

## CARNEGIE HALL PROGRAM

SEASON 1937-1938

FIRE NOTICE—Look around *now* and choose the nearest exit to your seat. In case of fire walk (not run) to *that* Exit. Do not try to beat your neigbbor to the street.

JOHN J. MCELLIGOTT, *Fire Commissioner*

---

CARNEGIE HALL

Sunday Evening, January 16th, at 8:30

S. HUROK

presents

(by arrangement with Music Corporation of America)

# BENNY GOODMAN

and his

# SWING ORCHESTRA

I.

"Don't Be That Way" .......... *Edgar Sampson*
"Sometimes I'm Happy" (from "Hit the Deck") .......... *Irving Caesar & Vincent Youmans*
"One O'clock Jump" .......... *William (Count) Basie*

II.

TWENTY YEARS OF JAZZ

"Sensation Rag" (as played c. 1917 by the Dixieland Jazz Band)
*E. B. Edwards*

PROGRAM CONTINUED ON SECOND PAGE FOLLOWING

---

The audience arriving at Carnegie Hall on the evening of 16 January 1938. The photograph in the center shows John Hammond's sister Alice (who became Mrs. Benny Goodman in 1942) and the respected jazz critic George Frazier. (Photo Eileen Darby, Graphic House)

Music News from Coast to Coast

# Down Beat

BALLROOM · CAFE · RADIO · STUDIO · SYMPHONY · THEATRE
608 S. Dearborn St.
Chicago, Illinois

Published Monthly

Subscription Price: U.S. $1.50 a Year—Canada $1.75—Foreign $2.00

Entered as second class matter May 25, 1936, at the post office at Chicago, Illinois, under the Act of March, 3, 1897. Copyright 1937, by Down Beat Publishing Co., Inc.

U.S. and Canada 15 Cents Per Copy

VOL. 5, No. 2       (Foreign 25 Cents)

CHICAGO, FEBRUARY, 1938

# Goodman Came, Saw, And Laid A Golden Egg

## Kyser Grit Molars As Idea On Their Brain Kids

## QUAKER CITY EXEC'S BLUSH AT PHONY HARMONY PACT

Philadelphia, Pa.—AFM execs here blushed recently when they discovered that the CIO musicians union had been fighting, finally signed a phony...

## Carnegie's Walls Bulge As 3 Klinkers & Sophisti-cats Hear

By H.E.P.

The Benny Goodman concert has been written into of swingology, for in Carnegie Hall on Sunday evening 16, 1938, the maestro came, played and laid a To some, the occasion was comparable to the disco- um, the feats of *les freres* Wright and Einstein's in his mathematical theories. Others linked it to t...annoying double-talk and Bank Night wi...

plus a set of ... The audience ... the strangest ass ... ered within the ... from a ...

---

PROGRAM CONTINUED ON SECOND PAGE FOLLOWING

# Carnegie Hall Gets First Taste Of Swing

## FEATURE NEWS

### Benny's Clarinet Sounds Good To Lorgnette's-Band A Bit Shaky

Chicago, February, 1938

By Annemarie Ewing

The boys were nervous. After all, it was Carnegie Hall and the pile of the red plush seats was still ruffled from contact with the devotees who had listened to the Beethoven Fourth Symphony and the Mozart Haffner Symphony and the violin of Georges Enesco playing the Saint Saens concerto that afternoon. Even the New York Philharmonic Symphony microphone still hung in austere silence twenty feet above the first rows of the orchestra.

And supposing you were Harry James or Gene Krupa or Babe Rus-sin, with a nervous grin on your face and the knowledge of a vast concert hall filled with 3900 people, more than a hundred of them sitting on chairs on the stage (at $2.20 a chair), and the space in the rear crowded with the dim shadows of people who had waited in line since ... o'clock that afternoon for ... to go on sale. ... for

graph of Wagner's dream of "Tann-hauser." They all recognized it—but Ivy called him "Vogner" to Philharmonic Sam's "Waggonner." When the sacred door was again locked, we heard music seeping through the dressing room section of Carnegie Hall—rhythmic, pul-sating music, not much like the kind that comes from concert meister's how.

It came from the sanctum sanc-torum of Philharmonic conductors, ... th ante room just ... me stair-

### Laying A Golden Egg In Carnegie Hall . . .

the violinist who ha... see what all the shoot a little wistfully, "an... chronizes!"
Then, all of a su... 8:45 and Benny, pa... was instructing every... together, and the boy... other around in the... about four square... photographers, m... holders with seats... curly-headed usher... dignified, and the ... boys refusing to be... And Gene asking... body in the hou... And Benny inst... Godfrey ("Benny... but mah name's... later at the S... boys from Elli... boys from Bas... he finished w... Happy." And ... being pushed to... plause welling... ing able to ... frey" (or ... leaned down... of Ber...

US

PROGRAM CONTINUED ON PAGE 12

The Carnegie Hall stage on 16 January 1938: Benny, members of the band, the dynamic Gene Krupa on his drums, audience overflow. Note that the audience, at least this group of them, were not teenage jazz 'addicts', but serious music-lovers – perhaps the 'sophisti-cats' referred to in the *Down Beat* article (left), which was far from complimentary towards the concert. *Down Beat* (above) gave a second version of the concert, this one with more 'human interest' and backstage reporting.

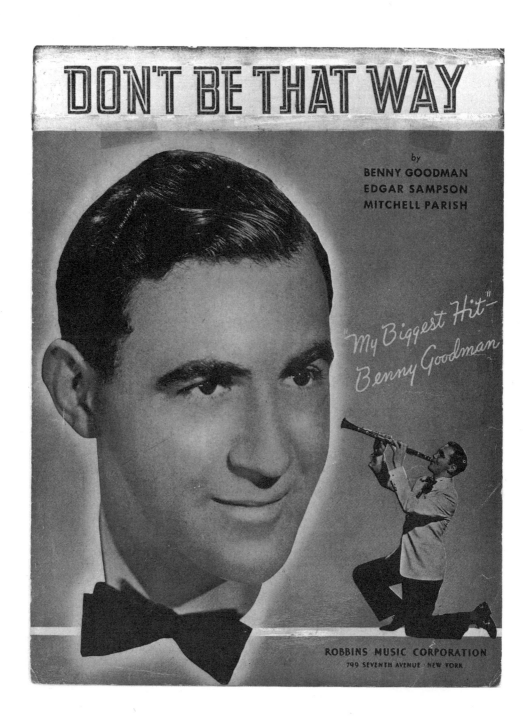

Sheet-music cover of a Benny Goodman hit, 1938.
This was the number with which Benny began the Carnegie Hall concert.
*Opposite :* **The original Trio rehearsing in the late 1930s.**
**Al Hirschfeld's deservedly famous cartoon of the Trio, on the
occasion of a performance they gave on the CBS television program**
*Omnibus,* **hosted by Alistair Cooke. The year was 1953.**

*Overleaf :* **Various shots of the Goodman Trio and Quartet. Benny's
small-group innovation was emulated by Bob
Crosby's 'Bob Cats,' Tommy Dorsey's 'Clambake Seven,' Woody
Herman's 'Woodchoppers,' and Artie Shaw's 'Gramercy Five.'**

Big Broadcast of 1938 Wants
Benny Goodman's Quartette

By John Hammond

...lmond could do was to sit in a corner
...roan, for the greatest asset of
...ease and subtlety, was
...ght.

6

FEATURE NEWS

# Hysterical Public Split Goodman & Krupa

## Gene Broke Contract, But B.G. Refused to Hold Him to It

By John Hammond

New York, N. Y.—A bombshell struck the orchestra world when Gene Krupa up and left Benny Goodman's orchestra. To the public outside Gene had become a symbol of the Goodman kind of music and it appeared to be unthinkable that Benny would ever allow Gene to quit. The whole story of the dispute is not entirely clear, and I will do my best not to add to the rumors which have already hit the press and musicians.

He is a master technician, an amazing good drummer when in the world. When he supplied much that immediately was something anything here. white bands... was the one of an in... it was he rushing and com... of guitar Allen rhythm on ... , and ... on ... ked ... ce ... In ... he ... ce ...

parting from the delicate style of the Fletcher Henderson arrangements which made the band revered by musicians the world over, Benny encouraged the exhibitionism of jungle drumming in works like Sing, Sing, Sing and many of the Jimmy Mundy "killer-dillers." These delicate little morsels promptly caused hysteria in audiences, and in more than one near-panic was initiated by the Goodman music.

Throughout this period Benny benefitted from Gene's showmanship and helped to make Gene famous. Gene's name was given featured billing, Benny secured him a date on Victor with his "own" band, was plugged on the air and became an American household ... highest what is ... American salari... signed ... th...

"Look what happen... press this ...

were a number of factors w... might not have occurred to m... cians, and it seems like a good i... to enumerate them.

Benny likes good, simple, relaxe... music, whether it is by Fletche... Henderson or Mozart. His idea, I'm sure, was to have a band modeled on that of Fletcher's golden group, which had more finesse than any... this country ever knew, and I be... lieve that he was distressed when he saw it drift into the easier bally... hoo style of lesser lights. He can... afford to have the band he wants right now, and I believe that you will find even more changes in his orchestral set-up very shortly.

B. G. On Edge Late...

The behaviour of his ... set the guy on edg... months. I har... third show ... recent ... to ...

*Opposite :* **The Goodman-Krupa split took place, amid maximum publicity, early
in March 1938, less than two months after the epoch-making Carnegie Hall concert.
Krupa formed a band of his own, but in later years appeared again with
the Goodman band to which he had contributed so much in the golden '30s.
Krupa died in October 1973, a victim of leukemia. His last appearance with the
Goodman Quartet was in August 1972.**
*Above :* **The great, sad Billie Holiday, with Teddy Wilson. Billie first appeared on
record with Benny in 1933, Teddy in 1934. (Photo Robert Asen – Metronome
collection)**

Rehearsal in 1937 : Benny, Martha Tilton and Vido Musso on the
saxophone. Musso left the band at the end of that year, joined Gene Krupa, then
Harry James, and returned to the Goodman outfit in 1941.
*Opposite :* 'The girls in the band.' Helen Ward, who was probably the band's
most reliable vocalist and the one who put over many of its biggest hits. *Top
right :* Anita O'Day, the stylish and highly polished singer who sang with the
Krupa and Stan Kenton bands, performed a number of times with Benny,
particularly during a European tour in 1959.
*Below right :* Martha Tilton (Photo Bruno of Hollywood)

*Opposite :* **Martha Tilton with Benny**
on one of their many theatre dates, **1938.**
Martha Tilton's association with Benny began
in August 1937 when she appeared on
a 'Camel Caravan' program, and her
last studio recording session with
the band was in 1958.
*Right :* **Mildred Bailey, a singer of great**
**and individual talent, whose voice can be heard on a**
**number of Goodman records.**
*Below :* **Red Norvo, Mildred Bailey's**
**husband, made a number of guest appearances on**
**Benny's radio shows, and joined the**
**band in 1944, then starring in Billy Rose's**
*The Seven Lively Arts.*
*Overleaf :* **Benny with the Budapest String**
**Quartet in 1938 when they recorded Mozart's** *Quintet*
*For Clarinet and Strings.* **(Photo Metronome)**

Publicity shot of Benny holding the Victor record he
made with the Budapest String Quartet. Note the photo used on the sleeve.
Joseph Szigeti, Bela Bartók and Benny Goodman in 1940 when they
were recording the Bartók composition commissioned by Szigeti and Benny :
*Contrasts For Violin, Clarinet And Piano*. **(Photo H. de Selmer Inc.)**

*Opposite :* **An informal chamber music session. (Photo Earl Theisen/Look)**
*Above :* **Legendary guitarist Charlie Christian (*left*) joined Benny in the summer
of 1939 and was one of a sextet that Benny formed at that time. Illness forced
him to leave in 1941 ; he died in March 1942.**

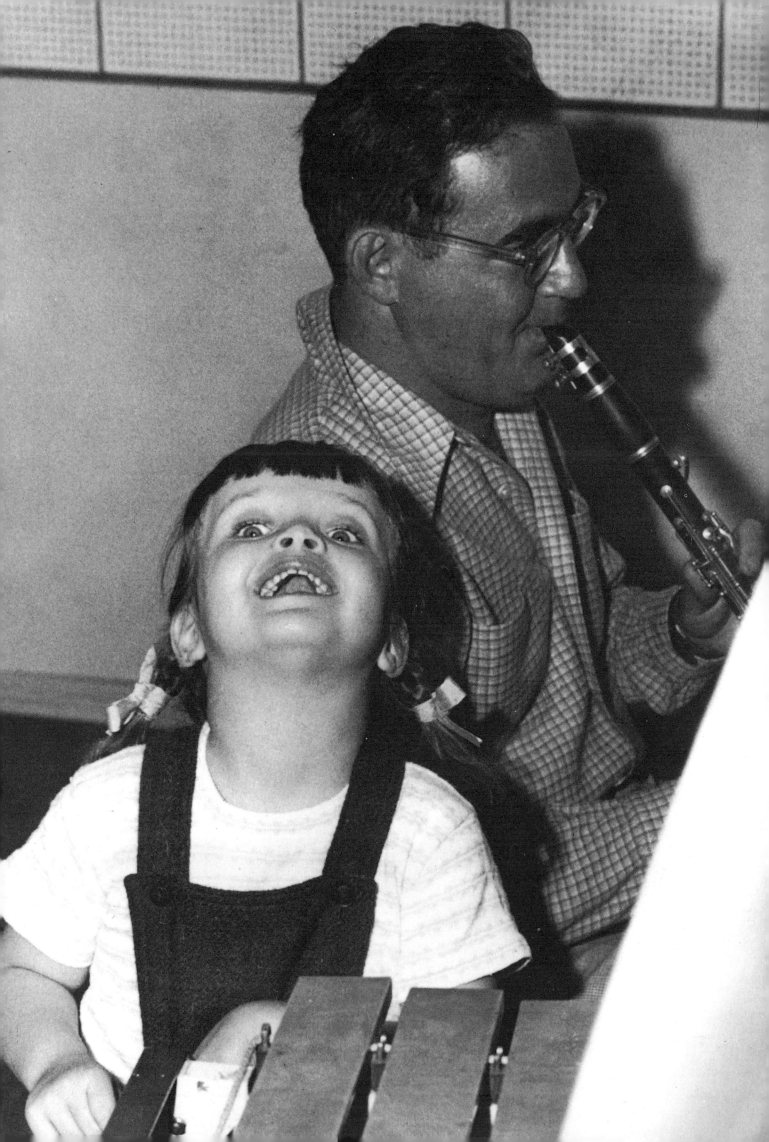

*Left*: **Benny with his elder daughter, Rachel,**
**inspiration for his recording,** *Rachel's Dream*.
*Below*: **Alice and Benny Goodman in 1945, three years after they were married.**

**The Goodman family; by now the second daughter, Benjie,
had joined the household. Benjie is remembered by the
Goodman band's recording of** *Benjie's Bubble.***(Photo Gene Lester)**
*Opposite above:* **Benny and Alice at Arrowhead Springs.**
*Opposite below:* **Rachel and Alice Goodman in the late 1950s.**

# MAKING MUSIC

**Benny Goodman and Leonard Bernstein**
**recording Bernstein's** *Prelude, Fugue and Riffs* **in 1963.**

A Benny Goodman Quartet performing at the U.S. Naval Air Station in
New Orleans, October 1944.
A cartoon of Benny around 1940 by Wachsteter.
*Right :* As early as 1952 *Down Beat* could write of the 'Swing Era' as
something of the past. By then television had captured the
fancy of the public.
Benny and a group, including Zoot Sims and Roy Eldridge,
during a European tour in the spring of 1950. (Photo Lindroos, Zürich)

# DOWN BEAT

VOL. 19—No. 24 (Trademark Registered U. S. Patent Office)
CHICAGO, DECEMBER 3, 1952
(Copyright 1952, Down Beat, Inc.)

## Cover Story

# Swing Era Lives Again In Great Goodman Album

**New York**—They rolled out the red carpet for swing again last month. The occasion was a celebrity-studded party at Columbia's New York studio to introduce a new album with a self-explanatory title: *Benny Goodman 1937-38 Jazz Concert No. 2.*

Album Rating: ★★★★★

**What happened at the party is described in pictorial detail on Page 9.**

What happens on the records is a result of the handiwork of Bill Savory, now a Columbia Records engineer, who in the 1930s was an ardent enough Goodman fan to take a large number of Benny's network broadcasts off the air.

These airchecks, after much careful sorting (half a dozen different takes were available on the same tune in several cases), have been assembled into two 12-inch LPs.

The album is lavishly produced, with close to 5,000 words of program notes by George Avakian. It starts out with Benny's opening theme *(Let's Dance)* and a short speech by Benny; it closes with the full famous radio-fadeout theme, Gordon Jenkins' *Goodbye.*

Of the 37 items presented, 21 are by the full band, the rest by the trio and quartet. There are only three vocals, one by Martha Tilton and Helen Ward.

This album represents a substantial addition to the Goodman collection in two respects. First, from the standpoint of jazz, the performances are technically excellent... Second, the numbers that were never...

There is more...

white. Suffice...

it was...

hea...

Left: **Teddy Wilson and Helen Ward during the tour in 1953 which Benny left after appearances in Boston and New York. Gene Krupa led the band for the remaining engagements, and Louis Armstrong and his All Stars were also part of the tour. (Photo Peter Basch)**
Below: **Benny, Teddy Wilson and Gene Krupa just before the start of the 1953 tour of a reconstituted Goodman band that included a few of the old gang, such as Ziggy Elman, Georgie Auld and Vernon Brown.**

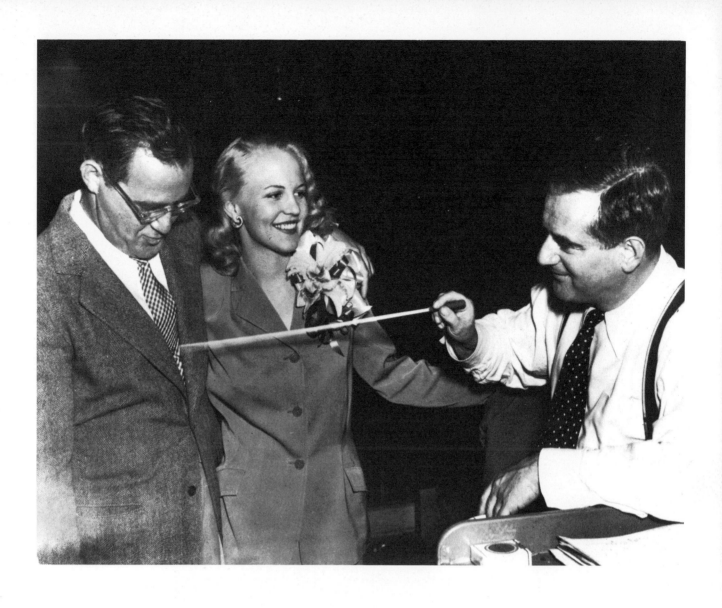

**Benny Goodman with Peggy Lee and Mark Warnow in the early 1940s.**
*Right :* **Benny and Peggy nearly twenty-five years later,**
**photographed at the Circle Star Theatre in San Carlos, California.**

*Opposite above :* **Back in 1948 Patti Page sang with a Goodman group on a number of radio broadcasts. In 1957 Benny returned the favor with a guest appearance on the Patti Page television show.**
*Opposite below :* **Mitzi Cottle sang with the band during an engagement at the Waldorf-Astoria in 1957.**
*Above :* **A cartoon of Benny in 1957.**

*Opposite above :* **Frank Sinatra and Benny changing roles during
a radio broadcast in 1943 when Benny was Sinatra's 'guest'. (Photo UPI)**
*Opposite below :* **Another example of
role-switching : Benny and Jack Benny in 1966. (Photo UPI)**
*Above :* **Benny with a straw hat, Maurice Chevalier
with clarinet, during an engagement at the Waldorf-Astoria in 1966.**

Teddy Wilson, Benny Goodman and Buck Clayton in Hollywood, 1955,
during filming of Universal-International's *The Benny Goodman Story*. **Of that
supposed biography, Benny says, 'Well, the music was good.'
A sketch of Benny by René Bouché.**
*Opposite :* **At the Newport Jazz Festival in 1958 : Benny with John Hammond.**

Benny with Eleanor Roosevelt in the 1950s. The
young couple beside Mrs. Roosevelt remain unidentified
(Sterling Hayden?).
Bone-fishing in Florida in 1956 with the baseball star
Ted Williams.
*Right :* The British jazz pianist, George Shearing, July 1954.

Fletcher Henderson in late January 1952 at a party given by Columbia to celebrate the release of 37 records taken from broadcasts by 'the old BG band.' The get-together included Helen Ward, Hymie Schertzer, Art Rollini and Vernon Brown.
*Right :* Benny with Count Basie and Sarah Vaughan in the 1950s.

*Left :* **Rachel as an infant.**
**Benny showing the girls how the clarinet works.**
**His efforts were unavailing ; Rachel eventually**
**chose the piano, Benjie the cello.**
**The Goodmans in about 1955 :**
**Sophia, Benny, Alice and Shirley. In front of them, Rachel and Benjie.**
**Sophia and Shirley are also named in Goodman recordings.**

Sheet music from the Warner Brothers release
of 1938, *Hollywood Hotel*, in which the Goodman band appeared.
Its 'Orchid Room' sequence is considered the acme of swing
music on film.
*Right:* Benny with the singer Frances Langford
in a publicity still for *Hollywood Hotel*. In 1950 Benny and
Miss Langford again collaborated for the NBC – TV series, 'Star
Time.'

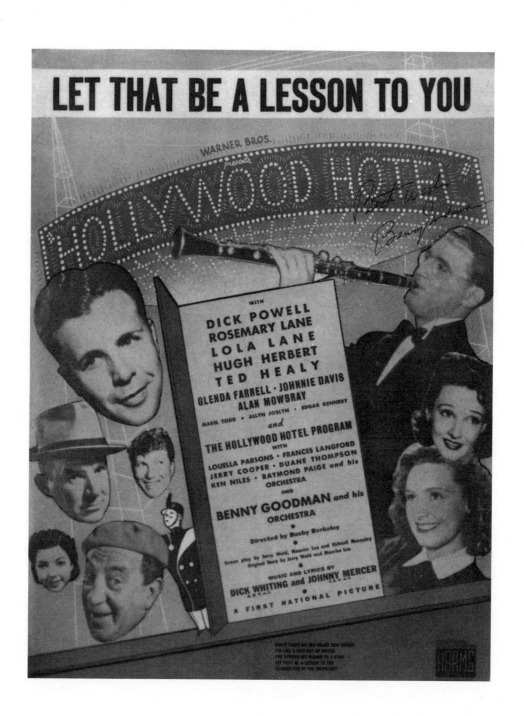

*Left :* **In** *Hollywood Hotel,* **the full orchestra, probably the best combination of the many that Benny assembled, did some five numbers, including** *Sing, Sing, Sing* **; and the original Quartet performed** *I've Got A Heartful of Music.*
**In 1942, the Benny Goodman orchestra appeared in a United Artists film called** *The Powers Girl.* **Of the old crowd only Hymie Schertzer was left. New stars were Jimmy Maxwell, trumpet ; Lou McGarity, trombone ; and Peggy Lee's husband, Dave Barbour, guitar.**

Three more of Benny's Hollywood ventures. *Below : The Gang's
All Here*, a Twentieth Century-Fox musical epic of 1943. Here Benny is seen with the
inimitable Brazilian bombshell, Carmen Miranda. Louis Bellson is at the drums.
*Sweet and Lowdown* (1944) was another Twentieth Century-Fox film which
featured Benny Goodman and his band. Jack Oakie, leaning up against the piano,
made many appearances on radio with Benny Goodman in the 1930s.
*A Song is Born* (1947) was a Goldwyn picture which
starred Danny Kaye and featured Louis Armstrong among other jazz musicians,
along with the Benny Goodman sextet.

*Below :* **Poster advertising an appearance in Amsterdam during the 1958 tour of Europe. During an engagement at the Waldorf-Astoria in March 1957 the band comprised Buck Clayton, Jimmy Maxwell and Nick Travis on trumpet, Frank Rehak and Rex Peer on trombone, Al Block, Sol Schlinger, Budd Johnson and Red Press on saxophone, Mel Powell on piano, Mousey Alexander on the drums, Steve Jordan on guitar and Irv Manning on bass.**

# NACHTCONCERT

PRESENTATIE LOU VAN REES

2 UREN LANG   Geen RADIO, geen T.V.

## 14 Mei 1958 · Concertgebouw · 11.30 uur

PLAATSEN: f 5.-, f 7.50 en f 10.-  belasting inbegrepen   AANVANG KAARTVERKOOP ZATERDAG 19 APRIL
bij de NIEUWE MUZIEKHANDEL, Leidsestraat, MUZIEKHANDEL CENTRAAL, Reguliersbreestraat en aan het CONCERTGEBOUW

# THE BIG BAND OF
# BENNY GOODMAN
# INCLUDING THE SEXTET AND THE QUARTET

Benny, Guy Lombardo, and a magnum of champagne.
Two leaders from the big band era:
Benny and Fred Waring, 1957. (Photo Bill Mark)
*Opposite:* **Benny showing a picture of Rachel**
when she was three weeks old to Vaughn Monroe and Woody Herman.
Paul Whiteman in June 1964 at the Disneyland Hotel in Anaheim, California.

On 6 September 1957 a Goodman group
performed at a United Nations Staff Day reception.
*Opposite :* The film actor William Holden joins Benny and
the band during a concert in the Grand' Place of Brussels in May 1958.
Benny's appearances at the U.S. Pavilion made it the Brussels Fair's
most popular attraction. (Photo Suzanne Szaszi)

SECRETARY-GENERAL

10 September 1957

Dear Mr. Goodman,

May I express to you the deep appreciation of
the United Nations Secretariat for your appearance
in the General Assembly Hall Friday last. Your
generous contribution to the success of the Staff
Day reception will be long and vividly remembered.

I send you most cordial regards.

Yours sincerely,

Dag Hammarskjöld,
Secretary-General.

Mr. Benny Goodman,
200 East 66th Street,
New York, N.Y.

united nations

staff day 1957

september 6

Rehearsal and performance
photographs of *Swing Into Spring*, a
television special which
featured Jo Stafford, Ella Fitzgerald,
Benny and the band, the McGuire
Sisters and Harry James (1958).

*Opposite :* Swing Into Spring **in 1959**
**included some of the same guests as the year before.**
*Below :* **Celebrating twenty-five years in show business :**
**Peggy Lee, Benny, Lionel Hampton and Ella Fitzgerald at '21' in New York (1959).**

Some Goodman alumnae. Cozy Cole on drums. One of the great
saxophonists, Zoot Sims. Buddy Greco played piano with the Goodman orchestra,
and also did some vocals, in 1948 and '49. Lou McGarity on trombone.
The young Stan Getz played tenor sax
with Benny at various times between 1945 and 1955.
'Mr. Five-by-Five,' Jimmy Rushing, another Goodman
star of the 1958 Brussels engagement.

Overleaf: **Harry James rejoined his old leader, Benny, in 1958 for** Swing Into Spring **on TV. Their association started in 1937, and even after James left to start his own band he often appeared with Benny on special occasions.**
Overleaf: **Louis Armstrong and Benny in 1953 before their projected road-tour went sour. (Photo David B. Heent)**

# WESTERN UNION
## TELEGRAM
W. P. MARSHALL, PRESIDENT

1201

The filing time shown in the date line on domestic telegrams is STANDARD TIME at point of origin. Time of receipt is STANDARD TIME at point of destination

LB540

1955 DEC 13 PM 10 04

L LLH640 - NL PD=TDL HOLLYWOOD CALIF 13=

BENNY GOODMAN=AR

200 EAST 66 ST NYK=

DEAR BENNY, HOPE YOU LIKE THE TRACK. JUST FOR KICKS I

MADE ANGELS SING TO PROVE I,M PART JEWISH. THANKS FOR

THE PLEASURE. SINCERELY=

HARRY JAMES=.

# CARNEGIE HALL

### SEASON 1952-53

Friday Evening, April 17th, at 8:30 o'clock

## JAZZ CONCERT

*by*

## BENNY GOODMAN and LOUIS ARMSTRONG
## BENNY GOODMAN and his ORCHESTRA and TRIO

Benny Goodman, *Clarinet and Leader*

*Saxophones*

Willie Smith ...........................................................alto
Clint Neagley ...........................................................alto
Georgie Auld ...........................................................tenor
Sol Schlinger ...........................................................tenor

**Program Continued on Second Page Following**

*Opposite* : **Martha Tilton at the 1958 Newport Jazz Festival.**

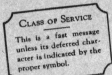

## WESTERN UNION
### TELEGRAM
W. P. MARSHALL, PRESIDENT

CLASS OF SERVICE

This is a fast message unless its deferred character is indicated by the proper symbol.

SYMBOLS
DL=Day Letter
NL=Night Letter
LT=International Letter Telegram

1220
(R 11-54)

(36)

The filing time shown in the date line on domestic telegrams is STANDARD TIME at point of origin. Time of receipt is STANDARD TIME at point of destination

= NA25 1 LONG DL PD=WUX NEW YORK NY 2 1204PME=

1957 JUL 2 PM 12 36

BENNY GOODMAN=

200 EAST 66 ST=

THE PARAMOUNT THEATRE CORDIALLY INVITES YOU TO BE A GUEST
OF HONOR AND TO SIT IN THE GOLDEN ROW OF STARS NAMED FOR YOU
THE NIGHT OF JULY 10 WHEN OUR THEATRE LAUNCHES ITS 30TH
ANNIVERSARY SUMMER FESTIVAL WITH THE WORLD PREMIERE OF
"BAND OF ANGELS" STARRING CLARK GABLE AND YVONNE DE CARLO=
PLEASE TELEPHONE MISS BENSON AT CIRCLE 6-1000, EXT= 222, SO
THAT WE CAN MAKE RESERVATIONS FOR YOU AND YOUR GUEST=

ROBERT K SHAPIRO MANAGING DIRECTOR PARAMOUNT THEATRE=

10 30 6-1000 222=

# An Evening with Benny Goodman

A CLASSICAL AND JAZZ CONCERT BENEFITING
THE NEW YORK UNIVERSITY MEDICAL CENTER

*Sunday Evening, March 17, 1968, at 8:00*

## Chamber Symphony of Philadelphia

ANSHEL BRUSILOW, *Conductor*

ROSSINI  Overture to "Il Signor Bruschino"

RAVEL  Le Tombeau de Couperin
    I  Prelude
    II  Forlane
    III  Menuet
    IV  Rigaudon

VON WEBER  Clarinet Concerto No. 2 in E-flat major, Opus 74
    BENNY GOODMAN

INTERMISSION

**Licia Albanese,** with the Chamber Symphony

PUCCINI  Si, Mi chiamano Mimi from "La Boheme"

PUCCINI  Un Bel Di from "Madame Butterfly"

VILLA-LOBOS  Bachianas Brasileiras No. 5 for Soprano and Celli

## Benny Goodman Septet

featuring
**Lionel Hampton–Teddy Wilson**

With Joe Newman, Gene Bertincini, George Duvivier and Bobby Donaldson

Finale—Entire Company in a Salute to George Gershwin

The taking of photographs and the use of recording equipment are not allowed in this auditorium.

Members
concert an

**SUMMER SYMPHONY XV**

**ARTHUR FIEDLER**
Conductor
**BENNY GOODMAN**
Soloist

and the
SAN FRANCISCO
SYMPHONY ORCHESTRA

Benefit of The Children's Health Council

RCA VICTOR STEREO VICS-1402

Benny Goodman *plays* Mozart
Clarinet Concerto, K. 622
Munch/Boston Symphony Orchestra
Clarinet Quintet, K. 581
*Boston Symphony String Quartet*

---

**Benny's classical performances and recordings.**
*Opposite left :* **Performing with the Boston Symphony
Orchestra under Charles Munch at Tanglewood, Mass., in 1956.
In 1947, Paul Hindemith wrote a Clarinet Concerto
for Benny, who commented of the work that it 'takes some doing'.**

---

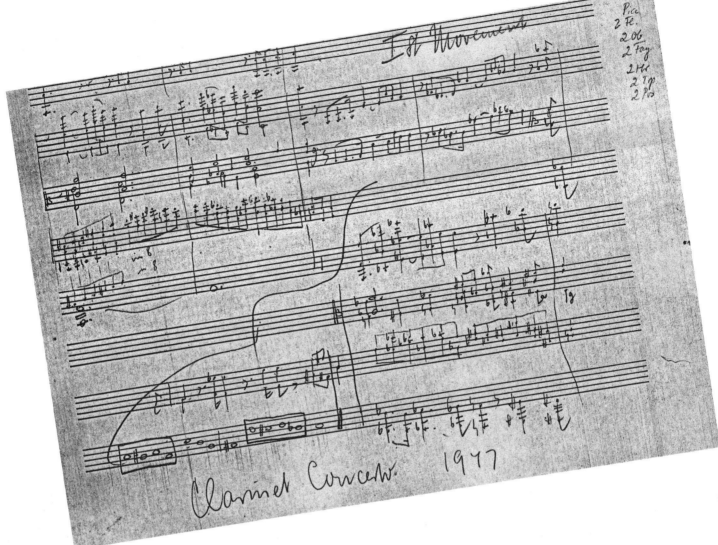

Benny poses at Basin Street East, New York, with five visiting Soviet
composers, 21 November 1959. On Benny's left is Dmitri Shostakovich. (Photo UPI)
Benny with the great Spanish cellist, Pablo Casals, in Puerto Rico.
*Opposite :* **The choreographer George Balanchine, the composer
Morton Gould, the clarinetist Benny Goodman : rehearsal for the ballet**
*Derivations***, 1964. (Photos Martha Swope)**

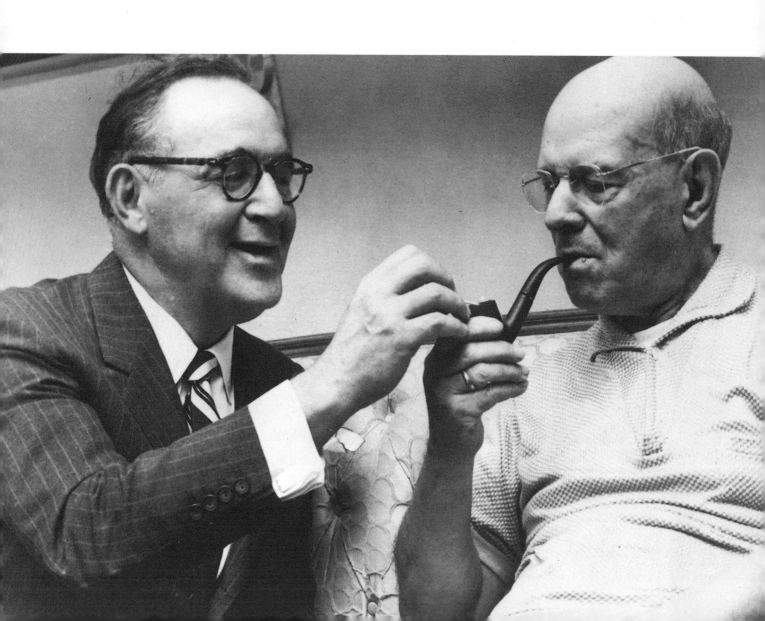

Recording session with Igor Stravinsky, 1966 *(below)*;
Morton Gould; Leonard Bernstein; and Aaron Copland.

*Opposite :* **Benny rehearsing with the French-horn player, Barry
Tuckwell, for a recital they gave together in 1978. (Photo Henry Grossman)
Benny as art-collector. The painting is Monet's**
*Cliff at Etretat* **; the sculpture is by Seff Weidl. (Photo UPI)
Benny photographed with an oil portrait of him by René Bouché. (Photo UPI)**

*Left :* **Stamford, Connecticut : the Goodmans' two hundred-year-old house.**
**(Photo Burt Owen)**
**Two of Benny's favorite forms of relaxation are fishing and golf. (Photo UPI)**
*Above :* **A family gathering at O'Hare Airport, Chicago, May 1962.**
**Behind Benny and his mother are his sister Ida and his brother Louis and wife.**

## Benny and daughter in 'Pop' concert

When veteran Benny Goodman, King of Swing, appears as guest clarinetist in a San Francisco Symphony Fiedler "Pop" concert, Friday, Aug. 23 at 8:30 in Oakland's Paramount Theater, his pianist daughter Rachel will be co-soloist with him.

Father and daughter will star together in the "Allegro" of Weber's "Grand Duo Concertante." Born in 1943 in Los Angeles, she has played the piano since she was four and has had periodic concert experience. Presently she is studying for a Ph.D. in literature at UC Davis.

Aside from other "Pop" numbers to be conducted by Arthur Fiedler, Benny Goodman will appear in a Weber "Concertino" and a medley of Goodman favorites such as "The Man I Love" and many more.

A second symphony Fie

**RACHEL GOODMAN**
Her piano, his clarinet

Benny Goodman, world ambassador of swing – disembarking in
Moscow, meeting Harold Macmillan and President Kennedy in
Washington, U Thant in Rangoon, and blowing in São Paulo,
Budapest and Moscow.

The band in Tokyo during the 1956 tour. The vocalist is Dottie Reid.
Benny introduces the fellows in the band to the King of Thailand, Phumiphol
Aduliej, in the King's Palace, Bangkok, 1956.
Benny the photography enthusiast in front of a temple in Bangkok.
*Opposite*: Benny and Alice visiting the Schwedagon Pagoda at Rangoon, 1956.

Benny presented a clarinet to the King of
Thailand, a jazz enthusiast, who during a later trip to
New York *(bottom)* jammed with Urbie
Green, Benny, Jonah Jones and Gene Krupa.
*Below :* A visit to the Japanese
Prince and Princess in Tokyo, January 1957.
*Opposite :* Benny rehearsing for a concert
performance with the Tokyo Symphony Orchestra,
February 1964; and appearing with
the Burmese State Orchestra in Rangoon.

*Opposite :* **During the Moscow trip : shaking hands with Khrushchev, entertaining children in Red Square. Bill Mauldin's cartoon emphasizes its propaganda value.**
*Above :* **Benny visits a synagogue in Tbilisi. (Photo LIFE)**

*Below:* **The original Quartet together again in 1972 for a television appearance in the 'Timex All Star Swing Festival'; other old friends on the show were Count Basie, Ella Fitzgerald, Duke Ellington (at far right) and Basie's vocalist Joe Williams beside him. Doc Severinson, trumpeter, was M.C.**
*Right:* **A get-together in Benny's Manhattan apartment to celebrate the 30th anniversary of the original Carnegie Hall concert (1968).**

**Benny in conversation with Princess Margaret in October 1976, when
Benny appeared at St. John's Smith Square, London, to play music by
Malcolm Arnold. (Photo Ron Galella)**

# WOODY ALLEN

October 5, 1972

Mr. Benny Goodman
200 E. 66th St.
New York, N.Y.

Dear Benny:

Enclosed are two photographs
of a particular Selmer, and an
album cover with a very fine looking clarinet on it.  What I want
to get is an old Selmer with a
swan's neck octave key and rollers
on the pinkie keys.  I'm not sure
the album cover photo is a Selmer,
but the ones in the photographs are.

I have one Selmer at home and
its fair, but not as responsive
as the cheap Italian clarinet that
I play now.  I believe either the
clarinet in the photographs or on
the album cover belonged to Jimmy
Noone and was a gift to George Lewis.

Hoping to hear from you soon
and best wishes.

CARNEGIE HALL
1978

*Opposite :* **Cartoon of Benny by David Levine, 1976.**
*Left :* **Cover of the 1978 commemorative
Carnegie Hall concert.**
*Below and following pages :* **Photos taken before and
during the concert, showing Mary Lou Williams
relaxing with friends, Benny in his familiar stance,
and Lionel Hampton exuding joy. Martha Tilton came
back to sing her old hits** *Loch Lomond* **and** *Goody-
Goody***.**

*Overleaf:* **Benny in 1978. (Photos Theo Westenberger)**